CW01500191

FRIENDS ABROAD

Memories of
Lawrence Durrell, Freya Stark,
Patrick Leigh-Fermor,
Peggy Guggenheim
and others

MAURICE CARDIFF

The Radcliffe Press
London · New York

Published in 1997 by
The Radcliffe Press
An imprint of I.B.Tauris & Co Ltd
Victoria House
Bloomsbury Square
London WC1B 4DZ

175 Fifth Avenue
New York
NY 10010

In the United States of America
and Canada distributed by
St Martin's Press
175 Fifth Avenue
New York
NY 10010

Copyright © 1997 by Maurice Cardiff

All rights reserved. Except for brief quotations in a review, this book, or any part
thereof, must not be reproduced in any form without permission in writing from the
publisher.

A full CIP record for this book is available from the British Library

A full CIP record for this book is available from the Library of Congress

ISBN 1 86064 221 7

Library of Congress Catalog card number: available

Designed, typeset and produced by John Saunders Design & Production
Printed and bound in Great Britain by WBC Ltd, Bridgend, Mid Glamorgan

Contents

Author's Note

I worked for the British Council from 1945 to 1973 in Greece, Italy, Cyprus, London, Mexico, Belgium, Thailand and France in that order. Other than in the first few pages of the introduction there is scarcely any reference to whatever work I may have done for the Council since in these memoirs I have confined myself to writing only about certain friends we were lucky enough to make while living abroad and who subsequently re-entered our lives in England or in other countries to which we were posted. The one exception is Osbert Moore whom we first met in England, but the sketch of whose life could not have been written without learning of his posthumous fame in Bangkok and Sri Lanka.

Introduction – Greece 1945

DURING the German occupation of Greece in the Second World War I spent some months with the communist resistance in the Aegean islands. After the German retreat I took on the role of political adviser to the British brigadier in command of the region. When the Greek army arrived in the islands in the spring of 1945, the brigadier lost his command. He had made his headquarters in Mitylene. One morning I waved goodbye to him from the quay as he made off in a naval motor launch accompanied by a central European cabaret dancer from Istanbul. Although I hoped the army might have forgotten about me, I realized it could not be long before my own recall. When it came I was summoned to Athens by Kenneth Johnston, a charming erudite colonel whom I had known in Cairo.

I left Mitylene sailing for the last time in the schooner which the brigadier had earlier passed on to me after he had been allotted a naval motor launch. I said goodbye sadly to the boat and its crew at the Piraeus. On arriving in Athens I went to the British military headquarters where the colonel had his office on the top floor. I found him stuffing files into a briefcase. I had imagined I had only been sent for because my work in the Aegean had come to an end and I was required for other military duties. Now, to my surprise, I found myself being asked to take over the running of an organization of which I had scarcely heard and which had nothing to do with the army.

The colonel explained that he had worked for the British

1

Council before the war and had been looking after its interests since his arrival in Athens. He had been recalled to rejoin it in London and was due to leave by plane within the hour. He wanted me, if I agreed, to take over as its acting representative in Greece.

While he talked he went on filling his briefcase. When he finally snapped it shut he led me down the corridor, still talking, to the lift. He was so intent on explaining the aims of the organisation that we made two flights from top to bottom of the building before getting out at the ground floor. He stopped in the entrance hall and asked me if I would accept.

I had tried to take in as much as I could of what he had told me, but three privileges he had mentioned which went with the post were what had most stuck in my mind: first, seconded from the army, I would be allowed to wear civilian clothes: second, I would have a flat of my own: third, I would be given a car and chauffeur. I accepted without hesitation. Smiling encouragement and with an assurance that everything would be all right the colonel ran down the steps and dived into the car which was waiting to take him to the airport.

I already had some civilian clothes provided by the British Consul in Izmir to enable me to travel through neutral Turkey on the Taurus express. It was fortunate as there was little to buy in the Athens shops. Though an odd garb, a light faun jacket and bright blue trousers, I lost no time in getting into it.

From a friend I learnt of a flat to let in a little chalet at the edge of the pinewoods on Mount Lycabettus. It had a splendid view across Athens to the Acropolis and the Saronic gulf. Its vine-covered terrace shared the same view but also looked out over the yard of a dilapidated farmhouse to the western flank of mount Hymettus. A high wall screened it from the north wind so that even in winter it was warm enough to sit out in the sun.

Now, as it was already early summer, I slept on a camp bed under the vine. Nightingales sang in the pines and owls hooted from the roof tops below. Every morning I was awakened at dawn when the shutters of the farmhouses were flung open. As they banged against the walls, scores of chickens launched themselves out of the windows and flumped squawking into the yard.

I had no difficulty in acquiring a car as the Germans had left behind a large number of vehicles from among which the army allowed me to make my own choice. I picked on an old Mercedes which lasted out the two years I was to remain in Greece, surviving battering journeys over potholed roads with only a few minor breakdowns.

Settled in as a pseudo civilian I began daily stints at the office which had been rented by the colonel before my arrival. There I was bombarded with letters from London, some helpful, some worryingly obscure, others advising me of the imminent arrival of additions to the staff either to assist me in Athens or to set up outposts in Salonica, Patras and elsewhere. As they arrived one by one in the weeks which followed, our financial commitments grew so alarmingly that I telegraphed to London declining responsibility for them until I was sent proper regulations and a trained accountant. These were promised but took some months to materialize.

At first very few Greeks visited the office, but of those who did, some presented me with difficult problems. One morning my secretary announced that Mr Russos, a well-known poet and translator of Shakespeare, had called to see me. She ushered in a distinguished-looking old gentleman with abundant white hair and a beard. He told me he had been a friend of the colonel and that it was in the hope that his successor would prove as equally fine a gentleman and as good a friend to the Greeks as he had been, that he had called to see me.

I mumbled suitably and asked what I could do for him.

He explained that like all poets he was poor. Because of his support for the left-wing resistance, the Germans had confiscated all his property. Since they had left, the only possession he had been able to recover was an open-air cinema which had been unused since the beginning of the war. With nowhere else to go, he had made his home in one of the box offices at the entrance. He had lived there in reasonable comfort until he had published a poem attacking General Scobie, the commander-in-chief of the British forces in Greece. The very next day the army had retaliated by installing a loose woman in the box office opposite the one which he occupied and had turned it into a brothel. The soldiers who visited it made such a noise shouting and singing that it had been impossible for him to sleep. Driven from his refuge he had been forced to take what rest he could on a bench in a public park.

His health had begun to suffer and he had had to abandon his translation of *Henry V* when half way through the last act. Had the colonel still been in Athens, doubtless he would have appealed to the general on his behalf. But he had gone. What was I going to do to help him?

I couldn't do anything about the general or the loose woman in the box office, but I was able to send him away with his spirits lifted by arranging for his *Henry V* to be published in the *Anglo-Greek Review*, a prestigious literary magazine edited by George Katsimbalis, the original of Henry Miller's 'Colossus of Maroussi'. It had been supported by the colonel and had its office in the same building as our own.

Next I had a visit from a group of architects. While the junior members laid plans and models out all over the floor, the seniors explained their project.

Though fanatically opposed to the German occupation they were such well-known personalities that it had been impossible for them to escape from Athens to join the partisans. Near to starvation though they often were, they had spent their time preparing plans for the transformation of Athens when Greece was liberated. Sadly, they had been received without enthusiasm at the British military headquarters. At the embassy they had been advised to call on me.

The scheme they now revealed was bold enough to propose the transfer of the Greek capital to Corinth. Athens freed from the squalid architecture of administration and commerce would be reborn as an international university for the study of world civilizations. The models on the right showed how they planned to build the campus at the foot of the Acropolis. Those on the left showed Corinth greatly enlarged with the canal widened and harbours the size of the Piraeus at each end.

As they packed up their plans and models I wondered whether the colonel with all his goodwill and diplomacy could have managed to send them away any less discouraged.

After our announcement that we had scholarships to offer, I had a visit from a member of a very rich shipping family in Chios whom I had known when I was in the islands. I naively supposed he had come for a friendly talk. That was how the conversation began, but he soon brought out the real reason for his visit. He had a son of university age whom he wanted to study in England. Hearing of our scholarships he felt sure that, good friends as we were, I would be able to arrange for the boy to receive one to study at Oxford. When I explained that the scholarships were only for postgraduates, he gave me a conniving smile and put his hand inside his bulky briefcase. As he fumbled, I wondered what the bribe might be; a Tanagra figure, perhaps, or a piece of old Venetian silver or, more crudely, a bag of Marie Therese gold dollars? But the package he drew out was not of a very promising shape. Informing me as he unfurled the newspaper in which it was wrapped that it was a speciality of his island, he triumphantly plumped on my desk a pot of mastic jam.

One of the colonel's last-minute instructions had been for me to find a building in the centre of Athens suitable for use as an Institute of Higher English Studies. Relieved at having a legitimate excuse for getting out of the office, I spent many hours driving around the city before I found a house in a good position, which with some adaptation offered the facilities required. The owner was asking the equivalent of fourteen thousand pounds sterling to be paid in gold. I had to draw the money from the bank in sovereigns which I took in a small suitcase to the lawyer's office where the deal was to be completed. We spent an agreeable afternoon drinking cups of Turkish coffee as we counted the gold and arranged it in little piles on the lawyer's desk.

As it turned out, the house, centrally sited as it was, proved a sound investment at a time when our financial masters at the Foreign Office preferred to rent, stuffily if short-sightedly declaring that they were not in the real-estate business.

[1]

An Expedition to Mistra with Peter Norton and Herbert Read

Although I had travelled widely before the war I had had neither the inclination nor the necessity to have anything to do with British embassies, but in the role bequeathed to me by the colonel I had often to turn to the Athens embassy for assistance or advice. While I always found them friendly and helpful my only complaint might have been that when harassed by awkward visitors such as the authors of the 'grand design for Athens', they tended to get rid of them by passing them on to me.

When I first took over it was in an interregnum between ambassadors. Rex Leeper had just left and his successor, Clifford Norton, was on his way. One morning I read in the newspaper that he had arrived. That evening in a nightclub I noticed a middle-aged English woman jitterbugging with uninhibited verve. She was wearing a bright blue silk dress patterned all over in white script bearing the message 'The Navy's Here!' Someone at our table told me that she was Peter Norton, the wife of the new ambassador.

Formerly the owner of a gallery in London specializing in the avant-garde, she had brought out with her two young painters, Lucien Freud and Johnny Craxton. It was her intention, she would announce in her forthright way, to set up, when her husband died, an artists' colony on the island of Poros. Of the two artists who came out with her Freud did not stay long in Greece, but Craxton fell in love with the country and eventually made his home in Crete. If she persisted in her idea of founding the colony, it never

6

came to fruition, since, contrary to expectation, she died long before her husband who lived to a great age.

At first I found her intense manner unnerving and it was some months before I got to know her well enough to feel at ease with her. Eccentric and self-willed, she had an impulsive drive and vitality, which could be overwhelming, but beneath it lay a warm and generous nature. The energy she put into her efforts on behalf of destitute Greek children and the sincerity of her motives made the sewing-bee-cum-church bazaar charities of most British embassies appear patronising and opportunist. She was too direct and outspoken not to make enemies who delighted in concocting scandals round her more unconventional exploits, but they were far outnumbered by her friends especially among the Greeks.

Shortly before I left Greece for good she invited Herbert Read and myself to go with her as her guests on a weekend trip to any place of our choosing. When she had convinced us that she really meant it, we decided on Mistra, the deserted Byzantine city in the Peloponnese famous for its churches decorated with frescos and mosaics. Peter approved our choice as she was as keen to visit the place as we were. Her cousin, who was staying with her, volunteered to go with us.

As the roads were in a very rough state it was decided that we should take the train as far as Tripoli. An embassy car would be sent on ahead to await our arrival with a chauffeur to drive us on over the last forty miles of our journey.

We left on an early train, our tickets bought and seats reserved. Once settled in our compartment, Peter pressed into my hand a purse bulging with drachmas from which, she said, I was to pay all our expenses including a stay overnight on our way back at a hotel on an island in the bay of Nauplia. I protested that she was being too generous, but she insisted that we were her guests and that she was going to pay for everything.

On our arrival at Tripoli we were surprised to see Greek soldiers fully armed manning the full length of the station platform. A young captain approached Peter and, after saluting, explained that because of the threat from communist guerrillas the general-in-command had ordered that she should be escorted back out of the region under military protection. When she protested and asked to speak to the general, he replied that it was impossible because he was ill in bed. Polite but firmly intent on carrying out his orders he led us through the station building to where, on the road outside, the embassy Daimler stood waiting with two armoured cars in front of it and two behind.

Confronted with this formidable convoy Peter gave in. No doubt Herbert and I failed to hide our disappointment, for just as we thought all was lost, her cousin came to our rescue. If she returned with the ambassadress to Nauplia, she questioned, would there be any objection to the two other members of the party continuing the journey on their own? The captain replied that his orders were only concerned with Lady Norton's personal safety. Encouraged by her cousin, Peter generously agreed that if we could find any means of getting there we should go on to Mistra by ourselves. There was a row of taxis outside the station. Two drivers whom I asked to take us refused because they thought the road too dangerous, but a third, after I'd agreed to a fairly heavy charge, accepted. We calculated that if all went well we would have a couple of hours at Mistra and return in time to catch the train to Nauplia, reaching the island hotel to join the others for dinner.

As soon as we had waved goodbye as Peter's convoy moved off, we got into our taxi and set out. While the driver appeared extremely nervous and remarked at every bend of the road that it was just the place for an ambush, Herbert's latent spirit for adventure had been stirred and I think he was disappointed that we completed the journey there and back without incident. We both regretted that our stay in Mistra had been too short for us to have seen as much of it as we would have liked, but had we delayed longer we would have arrived in Tripoli too late to catch the train to Nauplia. Our carriage was full of soldiers two of whom insisted on giving up their seats for us. Herbert who was wearing a beret which gave him a vaguely military air, sat beaming happily, reminded perhaps of the camaraderie, as expressed in his best-known poem, of army life in the First World War. At Nauplia we took a boat out to the island and arrived at the hotel as planned in time to join the others for dinner.

The next day a British naval launch was sent out to the island to take us to the Piraeus. As it was already late by the time we got back to the embassy, Peter invited us to stay for dinner.

Uncomfortably aware that the purse, which had been bulging when she had first pressed it on me, was now quite deflated with only a few coins inside, choosing a discreet moment I handed it back to her insisting that as nearly all the money had been spent Herbert and I should pay our share. Adamant, as when she had first given it to me in the train, she refused even after I pointed out that the taxi to Mistra had greatly added to the cost of the trip.

The next morning I got up early and went to a shop selling antiquities, where I bought a fine Mycenaean cup. I had it packed up and sent round to the embassy with a note of thanks. Hardly had the messenger left when Peter telephoned. She hadn't realized the purse was so empty when I'd given it back to her. Clifford – the mildest of courteous, old-fashioned diplomats from what I had seen of him – was furious. She was afraid I would have to pay my share. I pointed out that I'd already offered to do so twice. 'Well, you'll have to now,' she said. 'You have no idea how angry Clifford is! And will you tell Herbert he'll have to pay his share too.'

I baulked at this and told her that if she wanted Herbert to pay she would have to ring him up at his hotel and ask him, herself. Both my contribution and present received, she sent me a contrite letter of thanks again blaming Clifford for being so unreasonable. I was relieved at having paid my share knowing how much our taxi had cost. Apart from having had the chance to see something of the medieval splendours of Mistra, I felt that the trip had given me another very different glimpse into the past, for there had been about it, with the embassy Daimler sent to Tripoli in advance and a naval launch dispatched to bring us back to Athens, a touch, if no more than a touch, of the grand, freewheeling style of the all-powerful British plenipotentiaries of an earlier age.

I had no regrets about the Mycenaean cup as I owed Peter a present for the many kindnesses she had shown us since her arrival in Athens. As I look back over the years during which I was associated in varying degrees of closeness with seven different embassies (a subject, perhaps, for a book on its own), her personality stands out for it genuineness and lack of pretension. Although her impetuosity might at times have been undiplomatic, she was never gratuitously rude, though tactless sometimes in too obviously cultivating the embassy husbands in preference to their wives.

Typical of her was the children's party she gave in which she allowed the children to take the embassy over in a riot of wild games encouraged by her Abyssinian butler who whisked them round over the parquet floor on Persian carpets. When she spotted a child standing alone taking no part in the mayhem she asked him what was the matter. On his replying that he was bored, she promptly rang up his parents, told them he was behaving badly and asked them to come at once to take him away.

A year after we had moved from Athens to Milan, Peter wrote to tell us that she was driving back to England from Greece and hoped to see us on the way. She rang up on arrival and we invited her to lunch with her companion, but she accepted only for herself. After lunch in her usual direct manner she asked me if I would do her a favour. Imagining that like many travellers at the time she had been caught out by the currency restrictions and expecting to be asked for no more than a modest loan of Italian lire, I replied that I would be delighted to help her in any way that I could.

'Right!' she said. 'I thought you might let me borrow your car to drive back to England. It seems there's something wrong with the papers of our car and the Italians are threatening to impound it. If you were to take it over I'm sure as you're living here you'd be able to sort things out with the police.'

My refusal was as forthright as her request but she didn't seem to mind. It had been a long shot and she'd tried it on. She could hardly have been surprised when I turned it down. Fortunately, she and her companion managed to square the police themselves and were able to continue on their journey.

When we were next in London she invited us to dinner. As an enthusiast for the avant-garde in painting she showed us her latest acquisition, a picture by a young artist who composed his abstracts by riding over the canvas on his bicycle while the oils were still wet. There were other more arresting pictures on the walls, but I was attracted to a large glass-panelled showcase in the drawing room. It was filled with antiquities, most of them Greek, among which prominently displayed, though possibly only for the occasion, in the middle of the centre shelf I recognised my Mycenaean cup.

[2]

A Tour of the North with
Patrick Leigh-Fermor

Once the building I had bought had been adapted for use as the colonel's Institute of Higher English Studies, the staff to run it began to arrive, notably Rex Warner, its director, and Patrick Leigh-Fermor, his assistant.

Following the publication of the *Aerodrome* and the *Wild Goose Chase*, Rex had come to be considered one of the most promising of the younger English novelists. Handsome, rock-like in build and feature, he had the air of being solidly to be relied upon, even leant upon in a tight corner. Unfailingly affable, he proved a delightful and amenable colleague, while his distinction as a classical scholar and acclaim as a novelist gave a much needed lift to our standing in Athenian intellectual circles. Quick to spot the comedy in our not infrequently misplaced endeavours, the merest amateurs that we were, to live up to the high ideals in cultural diplomacy set by the colonel, he tempered our dismay at the worst of our failures by his deep and reassuring chuckle.

Perhaps it was this temperamental, even moral, lassitude which after all his early promise was the cause of his failure to progress as a novelist, leaving him without anything about which he felt strongly enough, even with the ease he found in the actual practice of writing, to provide him with the subject for a book. After one last rather feeble novel with a cricketing theme he turned to historical biography, but once he had landed a well-paid and minimally exacting post at an American university, he stopped writing altogether.

He astonished us by the ease and speed with which he could write admirable prose, assuring us that when writing his novels he had rarely to cross out a word or make any other correction. At a midnight contest in a taverna, given quite difficult rhymes, he and Paddy Leigh-Fermor produced passable sonnets within minutes, but Rex's was the more perfect and metrically correct. On such convivial occasions and on weekend expeditions he was excellent company especially after a bottle or two of his favourite Kokinelli, the pink, resinated wine of Atticca.

It was only gradually that I found it disconcerting that he seemed almost always to agree with anything which was said to him, and was ready to fall in with any proposal so long as it did not involve him in undue mental or physical exertion. While his genial manner made him irresistably likeable, I began to suspect that his rock-like appearance belied his true personality, for the better I got to know him the less certain I became that he had any firm convictions about anything or any principles which, in pursuit of the line of least resistance, he might not have been ready to discard.

Paddy was in many ways the precise opposite of Rex for there was nothing rock-like about him to encourage anyone to suppose that he might be casually leant upon, nor in any other respect was his outward appearance deceptive. Byronically handsome, with a restless vitality in speech and action, even if one had not known of his daring wartime exploits, he had a bravura about him, a readiness to take on anything mentally or physically, which left no doubt of his being able to prove, if needed, a sterling champion.

Expelled from King's School, Canterbury, for an indiscreet but, by his own account, innocent attachment to a pre-Raphaelite beauty in a greengrocer's shop (after fifty years still a perennial topic, as I have heard on clerical authority, over teacups in the cathedral close), he studied for a year under a congenial and enlightened tutor, acquiring without recourse to a university a wide-ranging scholarship which later in numerous subjects was to become profound.

With the intention of dedicating himself to a career as a writer he moved into lodgings in London's Shepherd Market, an area in itself not conducive to settled endeavour. Nor did his fellow lodgers give him any encouragement as they made the house the scene of endless wild parties into which, his plans for authorship indefinitely postponed, he threw himself with delighted, if reckless, abandon. When funds ran low and post-party gloom set in, with a typically romantic gesture he decided to break free from his London life to walk across Europe to Istanbul. He started out with only a few pounds in his pocket and with arrangements for an odd pound to two to be sent to await him in various cities on his chosen route. The journey successfully completed, he moved on to Greece and settled for a time, nearly penniless, in Poros. A magpie of a linguist he had picked up several languages on his travels and quickly became fluent in modern Greek. When the war came he joined the British Army, serving on the Greek mainland and later in Crete, where he famously abducted a German general and carried him off to Egypt in a submarine. His military service over, he was recruited into the British Council by the colonel who foresaw what a valuable asset he could be in Greece with his knowledge of the language and his renown as a hero of the Greek resistance.

The arrival of Rex and Paddy was followed by that of our officially appointed representative, Steven Runciman, the immensely distinguished historian. I was then relegated to the role of his acting assistant. This came as a relief since I had begun to feel sole responsibility for our ever increasing staff worrying. I had, also, to cope with the innumerable packing cases containing all kinds of materials which were constantly being shipped out to us from London. Among these was a vast consignment of British government service lavatory paper which, with its harsh texture, when displayed for use, prompted aggrieved protests, especially from our Greek colleagues and visitors.

As we had recently set up an outpost in Salonica, Steven decided that Paddy and I should fly there to see how it was progressing. Joan Rayner, who was attached to the army information service, went with us.

Following their expulsion from the outskirts of Athens, the communist guerrillas had retreated to the north. Army information officers reporting their growing influence among the local population had suggested that it might be useful if we were to establish minor outposts in the region. Accordingly it was agreed that while we were in the north we should make a tour to include some of the more important towns so as to assess what might be done.

On our arrival in Salonica we booked in at the Ritz Hotel. At that time all the hotels were grotty and we only chose the Ritz because it sounded the grandest. During our stay we became friendly with the Russian barman. He was probably a communist spy but he entertained us with fantastic stories of his escape out of Russia during the Revolution. He had such a dubious assortment of bottles at the back of the bar that we resisted his efforts to tempt us to try his vodka and whisky, preferring to keep to the local raki, which we knew to be relatively harmless. But drink wasn't all that he had to offer. Once he had decided that, though civilians, we were too disorganized to be fellow spies, he brought out for our inspection the samples of cocaine and hashish he kept under the counter. It was, of course, years before the drug scene surfaced and became a problem the world over. The cocaine had no appeal for us but the hashish had romantic associations. Spurred by Baudelairean fantasies and feeling dare-devils, Paddy and I, while Joan mildly disapproved, bought a minute green block of what the barman assured us was the best *to mavro* to be had on the market.

Pocketing the little green block we went up to my bedroom. We fixed two amateurish joints, stretched out on the twin beds and started to puff away conscientiously. Joan, who sat watching us, complained that we ought to have gone out to eat first. She was a wonderful person to travel with, though rather given to moaning. This time she needn't have worried. Inhale as deeply as we could, the joints had no effect unless it was to make us giggle but, then, we found the situation comical and kept joking about it.

Afterwards, on our way out to dinner, we protested to the barman. He said it was our fault for being stingy. We should have bought two blocks instead of sharing one between us. Would a double dose have wafted us from giggles into a Baudelairean dream-world? We doubted it and were not tempted to try his wares again.

We stayed for a few days in the city before setting off on our tour over the rubble roads of the mountainous north in an old army vehicle, a kind of half-open barouche with seating for twelve. As we drove along, gifted raconteur as he was and still is,

Paddy told marvellous tales of his war and peacetime adventures, their climaxes often culminating as I heaved the barouche round a perilous hairpin or scraped the rock face on one side of the road to skirt a chasm on the other where a landslide had taken a bite out of the surface. Sometimes envy would question, 'Could that one really be true?' and compliant doubt would reply 'Surely not.' But on two occasions doubt was properly confounded.

We were taking a break in a village not far from the Albanian border. To stretch our legs we went for a stroll up the village street. Suddenly Paddy stopped. It had all come back to him. 'We'd just got here from the south. The Greeks, who'd beaten up the Italians, had been overwhelmed by the Germans. The army was in retreat, the soldiers heading towards the village in a disorderly rout. We tried to halt them to take a stand. In the middle of it all I spotted a white flag being hoisted on the bell-tower of the church. With one of the villagers I ran back and caught the Papas in the act and . . .'

He was interrupted. Our arrival had caused a stir in the village and some of its inhabitants had followed us. Now one of them breaking away from the others ran forward and clasped Paddy in a comradely embrace.

'Do you remember the day when the Germans were coming and the Papas put up a white flag and we grabbed the old bastard and made him pull it down?'

It was not until towards the end of our tour that doubt was finally silenced. Again we had stopped for a break, this time in a Thracian village under the Rodopi mountains. As we sat in the sun at a roadside café, Paddy was prompted to a reminiscence. 'I've been to this place before. It was during the Venezelist revolution. We had ridden down from the Bulgarian border and stopped here for the night.'

Scarcely were the words out when a man rose from a nearby table and stopped in front of Paddy with arms outstretched and a grin of recognition. 'Welcome, my friend! Do you remember that evening we spent together during the Venezelist affair? I can see you now as you came riding into the village wearing white Bulgarian boots!'

It was the white Bulgarian boots which clinched it. From that moment I believed retrospectively, beyond question, everything he had told us, for it was not only with his adventures that he had enlivened our journey but with his knowledge of Greece and the Greeks, their history, customs, folklore, songs, literature and language, this last including several regional dialects. He had a passion for words. Whenever we stopped, if in conversation with the local people he caught a word he hadn't heard before, he would question the speaker about its precise meaning and speculate as to its origin.

Like all fine linguists he could keep languages stored in his head to be brought out effortlessly though unused for years. Crossing a high pass over the Pindos range we came on some Vlach shepherds with their flocks. The Vlachs are said to be the remnants of a Roman army cut off by the invading barbarians. The survivors had taken refuge in the remote mountain area keeping their identity as a distinct clan and speaking a Latin-based language similar to that of the Romanians. Paddy had picked up Romanian on his travels. Now he tried it out on the Vlachs with some success in general conversation and triumphantly in an extended haggle over the purchase of a magnificent black goatskin cloak from one of the shepherds.

Our tour over, we returned to Salonica and after a cannabis-free night at the Ritz flew back to Athens.

With all his intellectual accomplishments and the sophistication he had acquired from the varied encounters on his trans-European walk, Paddy was still given to outbursts of spontaneous, youthful enthusiasm which, exciting him to over-demonstrative gestures or blinding him to hostile reactions, could result in his quite thumpingly putting his foot in it.

On the evening of our return from the north we joined some friends in the bar of the Grande Bretagne. These included Nico Ghika, the artist, and his wife Tiggie who, though they were to become friends later, had taken a dislike to Paddy on first meeting him. In recounting our adventures Joan mentioned the Vlach shepherd's cloak and begged Paddy to fetch it from his room to show it off. Happy to do so he returned in a few minutes with the cloak over his arm. When close to us he unfurled it and adopting a Byronic stance flung it round on to his shoulders. Unfortunately, as it whirled through the air, it caught all the drinks on the table and swept them pell-mell into Tiggie's lap.

16

By the time I next visited Salonica, Paddy had left Greece and, of course, Joan had left with him. He had not got on well with Steven Runciman, though, as with Tiggie, they were later to become friends. Personally, I was terrified of Steven. Friendly and charming though he was at our first meeting, I was prompted to attach a mental label to him; 'handle with care'.

No doubt, despite this precaution, I must have made blunders enough, grammatical, social, political and of every possible kind to make him often wince, but there were two early perceptions on my part which helped to smooth our relationship. The first was a matter of tact. Steven was already at work on his great history of the Crusades. When needing to consult him in his office, before entering I would open the door a little just long enough for him to put aside the 'Crusades' and replace it with some workaday file on his blotter. The second was more important. In response to any proposal I might make to him he always said 'yes'. But he had two kinds of yesses, one short, even clipped, was a true affirmative; the other, long drawn out with a dip in the middle, signified 'no'. The distinction was lost on Paddy, who on the strength of the longest of drawn out 'yeses' would set out on a six- week tour of the islands or a trip round the Peleponnese. Though a sad loss to us, all turned out for the best. Temporarily exiled from Greece, he and Joan made off with a photographer friend to the Caribbean, a venture which inspired him to write *The Traveller's Tree*, the first and one of the best of his travel masterpieces.

We did not see him again until five years later in Cyprus when, his distinction as a writer already assured, he was commissioned by a Sunday newspaper to report on an earthquake which had badly shaken the island and partially wrecked the town of Paphos. He sent a telegram inviting himself to stay and asking me to hire a taxi to take him to the scene of the quake. When he arrived I decided to go with him as far as Limassol.

The driver of the taxi turned out to be a handsome Turk with oiled black hair, olive skin, flashing black eyes and with the overall air of having landed moments before straight off the Central Asian Steppes. At Limassol, when ordered to stop outside the hotel at which I was to spend the night, as he opened the door for me, giving an extra flash of his eyes and displaying his white teeth in an insinuating grin, he brought out the one word '*Gabarez?*' as if it was a magic abracadabra opening for us, if we so wished, the doors of a harem worthy of a Turkish sultan. All the spark went out of his lurid anticipation as Paddy waved goodbye to me and ordered him to drive on through the night to Paphos.

Some months after Paddy's visit I had to engage a chauffeur. The only applicant who turned up for interview was the 'Turk off the Steppes'. As Hussein had proved an excellent driver and spoke reasonably good English, I decided to take him on. At first he was entirely satisfactory. Apart from driving well he was punctual, reliable, and kept the car in good order. He even offered to take over the garden without asking for an addition to his wages. He tidied it up as much as we allowed him to; for we liked its romantic wildness; and planted the borders beside the path leading from the road to the front door.

We had already been long enough on the island to have many visitors including such notables as the head of police, the chief justice and the governor himself. Approaching and leaving the house they had to walk between the rows of Hussein's plants which grew taller and bushier as the summer came on but showed no sign of serious flowering. When questioned about them he would murmur 'Beautiful blooms!' But the blooms never appeared. One morning we went out to find that, head-tall as they had been, the plants had disappeared, cut down to the roots. Questioned, Hussein smiled his flashiest smile, shook his head and sighed 'No blooms this year,' and he pointed to the sky as if the plants failure to bloom had had something to do with the weather.

Soon afterwards his good qualities became less evident. He was no longer punctual or reliable and he lost all interest in the garden. His manner became vague and during the day he often seemed to be half-asleep. Finally his driving became so erratic that I was reluctantly forced to dismiss him.

At the time I hadn't thought of making any connection between the plants Hussein had cut down when they failed to bloom and the little green block Paddy and I had bought off the barman at the Ritz in Salonica. It was later in London that summer that I was enlightened as to the trick he had played on us, when taken by Joan and Paddy for drinks with a friend who lived in Tangier. It was a warm evening so we sat outside on the terrace at the back of the house. Growing in a pot beside me I noticed a tall feather plant, unmistakably of the same species as those which Hussein had grown beside our garden path. When I asked what it was, our host, once assured by Paddy of my discretion, confessed that it was cannabis which he was cultivating for his own use.

The Traveller's Tree, published in 1950, had excellent reviews and won the Somerset Maugham prize for young writers. The award led to one of Paddy's most notorious gaffes which he delighted in recounting himself. The great tale-spinner, informed by mutual friends that his prize author was a guest at a villa in the south of France near his own, invited him to stay. Maugham suffered from an embarrassing impediment in his speech about which he was highly sensitive. During dinner on the evening of his arrival Paddy appalled his fellow guests by telling the story of a comical misadventure that had overtaken a friend due to his stutter which, at the climax, impervious to warning kicks under the table, he faithfully, but unthinkingly mimicked. Maugham, deeply offended, later conveyed a message to him through his butler that he was no longer a welcome guest and must leave the next morning.

Unlike Rex Warner who wrote so easily but stopped writing so early in his career, Paddy wrote and still writes with difficulty and extremely slowly, while always quick to grab at an excuse for abandoning any work in progress. Joan, without whose devoted support it is questionable whether he would have ever completed anything to which he set himself, claimed that in her efforts to keep him writing she had sometimes been driven to locking him up in his study. Whether this was true or not, when we stayed with them in the early seventies it was already eight years since the publication of his last book which, with those preceding it, had established him as the leading travel writer of his time. Despairing of his ever finishing the work he had then in hand, she spoke nostalgically of 'the years of fame' and told us how dismayed she had been when, after he had kept to his study for unusually long and uninterrupted spells, he had emerged one morning to announce that he had just completed the translation of a P. G. Wodehouse novel into modern Greek.

While he was easily diverted from his writing, being by nature gregarious and always ready for a trip to Athens to see friends and when in England enjoying a round of parties, balls and country house visits, Joan, with her blonde good looks, intelligence that matched his own and gift for friendship, was happiest in the company of people she was close to, especially her brother, Graham, whose temperament was very similar to hers.

During the barren years that followed the publication of *Rumali*, apart from these social distractions, he had allowed himself to be diverted into a project which, if it kept his admirers impatient for his next book, astonished his friends with yet another example of his remarkable versatility.

Although it would be impossible to be envious of someone so generous-spirited as Paddy and so totally lacking in envy or malice himself, it might be forgiven to wonder if it was quite fair that he should have been able to add to the long list of his other attainments – intrepid traveller, scholar, multi-linguist, courageous man of action, writer of genius – that of distinction as architect and designer.

After their extensive travels in Greece he and Joan decided to build themselves a house close to the village of Kardamyli on the southern coast of the Peleponnese. The site they chose, first seen from the steep hill above it, was a piece of land planted with cypress and olives, set a little back from the sea, but with a secluded cove for bathing below it. What had most attracted them was the superb view across the Messenian gulf to the mountains of the Pylos peninsula, scenically perfected by the sentinel cypresses in the foreground and a small island in the middle distance.

Unlike the modern seaside villas in Greece, far from being a blemish on the, then, almost unscathed coastline, the stone-built, tile-roofed house of Paddy's plan and design, influenced by, though not modelled on, the foursquare mansions of the pashas and agas of the Ottoman past, not merely looks as if it ought always to have been there but gives a focus to the beauty of its natural setting.

On the seaward side of the house he planned at varying levels numerous broad terraces. Into the surface of these he wove arabesques in a variety of stones and pebbles. In places the terrace walls curve round to form semicircular seats each giving a different prospect of the view across the gulf and, where shaded by trees, offering perfect sites for alfresco meals.

The outstanding feature of the interior of the house is its grandly proportioned book-lined room with tall windows on one side overlooking the sea and at one end – a distinctly Turkish touch – a projecting window, its rectangular recess furnished with a broad divan on which it would have been easy to imagine a rotund pasha sitting, hubble-bubble at hand, toying with his favourite concubine while listening with half an ear to the pleas of his impoverished and over-taxed subjects.

The book on which Paddy was at work during our visit, published in 1977 under the title *A Time of Gifts*, was conceived as the first volume of a trilogy describing his teenage walk across pre-war Europe. The second volume, *Between the Wood and the Trees* appeared in 1986. The third, at the time of writing, has yet to be completed.

Although he had diaries to help him, it might have been considered unlikely that in recounting that youthful adventure forty years on he would have been able to catch the carefree, romantic enthusiasm which had inspired it. That he was so successful in doing so, producing two masterpieces of travel writing even more warmly acclaimed and more widely enjoyed than his previous books with their more specialised subjects, was mostly due to his having kept over the years those same qualities, though backed by a surer scholarship, which had first set him out on his travels. It is this exuberance of spirit, this sustained questing after knowledge and this readiness to take life on and get the best possible enjoyment out of it for himself and for others who happen to be with him, that has made him the brilliant writer he is and the most engaging and stimulating of companions.

[3]

Lawrence Durrell
in Cyprus

When the army remembered me again it was to order me to leave for England to be released from its tentacles. I returned to Greece soon afterwards in the same role as before though no longer Steven's 'acting' assistant but the real thing. Leonora and the children, Charles and David, after an arduous journey by rail and ship, joined me a few weeks later. We moved into a modern suburban house, the best accommodation I could find, but which had little to recommend it other than its view over the plain of Kifisia to the mountain beyond.

It was during this second year in Athens that King George, following a referendum, returned from Exile in England. Marooned in his palace for his own security, bereft of his English mistress and friends and acutely bored by his Greek subjects, he ordered his equerry to round up for audience any British residents whose conversation might be likely to entertain him. Among those summoned were Rex Warner and myself.

Our reception at the palace was as cool as if the King had already decided that we were not at all the sort of Englishmen that he wanted to meet. Gestured towards straight-back chairs, we sat down and waited for him to start the conversation. But he didn't say anything. The silence lasted so long that I decided to break with court etiquette by speaking first. I told him I had been with the resistance in the Aegean. The people had had a hard time under the Germans. On some of the smaller islands they had come near to starvation.

He was not impressed. 'From what I've seen of the Greeks so far,' he said, 'they seem to be very well off.' Then, raising his hand and parting his thumb and forefinger fractionally: 'When I was staying a Claridge's, I got that much sugar with my coffee. Now I get all the sugar I want.' Silence. The King said nothing. Rex said nothing. I tried again to break it. I told him I had just come back from Corfu which I knew had been his favourite summer resort. I recalled how attractive the old town had been before the war. It was sad that much of it had been destroyed.

'So you were there before the war, were you: I hope you weren't a friend of that terrible fellow Durrell.'

I gave up. I wasn't a friend of Durrell's. I hadn't even met him. I had read and much enjoyed *Prospero's Cell*, an account of his life in Corfu in the 1930s. I was tempted to ask why he thought Durrell so terrible but felt it wiser to desist. We sat on in silence until the King made a vague wave of dismissal. We were relieved to escape.

At that time, Lawrence Durrell was running the British Army Information Office in Rhodes. Paddy, on a tour of the islands, had visited him. He had come back with an enthusiastic account of his entertainment in the flower-filled courtyard of Larry's house. They had had a wonderful time together. His charming and beautiful wife, Eve, had cooked marvellous meals and had looked delightfully decorative sitting at Larry's feet while he talked.

Some months later, Larry and Eve came over to spend a few days in Athens. I met them for the first time in a taverna in the Plaka. Apart from George Katsimbalis, an old friend of Larry's, I do not remember who else was in the party. The evening being warm and the moon full, we sat outside in the open air. Katsimbalis with his impressive bulk, the moonlight shining on his bald, domed head, dominated one side of the table. Larry sitting opposite him, short as to be almost dwarfish, head rather large in proportion to his body, eyes small but vibrantly intelligent, had taken on the role of cheerleading disciple at the feet of the master. He kept encouraging Katsimbalis as soon as he had finished one of his extravagant stories to start on another. This imbalance between them produced the impression of the table being on a slant, but if sloping down towards Larry, its tilt appeared even more marked towards Eve. Though not sitting at his feet, as Paddy had described, but on a chair beside him, for all her oriental beauty – marvellous dark eyes, dusky, rose-tinted complexion – her apparent acquiescence to being left out of the conversation made it seem that she was on a lower level than he was.

The evening was not altogether a success. Like most raconteurs, Katsimbalis was at his best when his stories rose naturally out of the conversation. Plied by Larry with 'Tell us that one about the very thick cat which saved your life in the Bulgarian war' or 'about that coprophagist friend who fed his mistress with ripe figs,' the Colossus complied but with less than his usual panache.

Towards midnight the story-telling came to an end. In the talk which followed, Larry proved how entertaining he could be himself. A purveyor of amusingly crazy notions and outlandish paradoxes, his pungent tone was accompanied by a disarmingly cosy chuckle. If, with his oddly proportioned physique, he had a hint of the satyr about him, it was difficult to imagine why King George, who had never set eyes on him, should have been so convinced that he was such a 'terrible fellow'.

It was already dawn when the party broke up. Enjoyable though it had been, it was uncomfortable to reflect that while the rest of us had talked, the beautiful Eve, so far as I was aware, had hardly spoken a word.

I saw him again two or three times during his visit. After he had returned to Rhodes he sent me a pamphlet autographed by Henry Miller which set out to prove that Marlowe wrote Shakespeare. This was followed by a minute book of his own poems printed on the Army's printing press. At Christmas he sent a card with another poem. After I left Greece in 1947 we temporarily lost touch.

It was not until 1953 when we were living in Cyprus that I heard from him again. He wrote from the embassy in Belgrade. He had resigned his post in the information department and wanted to know if I would recommend Cyprus as a place to retire to while writing a novel. He had saved enough money to get by for a year without doing any other work provided the cost of living was reasonably low. I replied that it was a beautiful island, that he should be able to live quite cheaply, but that he must remember that it was a British colony and not expect it to be like Greece. He wrote back that he had decided to come. He arrived a few weeks later without Eve, alone with his two-year-old daughter, Sappho.

Disaster had struck on the journey from Belgrade. On arrival at Trieste, Eve had had a breakdown. A British Army medical officer in the town had recommended that she should be sent to England for psychiatric treatment. This had cost so much that he had used up almost all the money on which he had intended to live while writing his novel.

He had arrived while we were away on holiday. By the time we returned he had already settled in Kyrenia, an attractive town on the north coast of the island. So much worse off than he had expected to be, he had taken rooms in a modest Greek Cypriot house. At first he looked after Sappho entirely by himself. She was a beautiful child with Eve's dark eyes and complexion. Considering what must have been a traumatic separation from her mother, she appeared, at least on the surface, to have been remarkably undisturbed by it. If she settled down quite happily in their rather stark surroundings, it must have been largely due to the patient care which Larry devoted to her. That he should have been a loving father to such an attractive child was not surprising, but I would not have predicted, from what I had seen of him in Athens, that he would have been capable of taking on the role of her absent mother with such tenderness and efficiency.

As it was no longer possible for Larry to live on the island without working, I gave him an introduction to the headmaster of the Pan-Cypriot Gymnasium, the prestigious high school for children of the Greek Cypriot community. Fortunately the school had need of a Greek-speaking English teacher. His interview with the headmaster went well and he was offered the post at a reasonable salary. Starting in the early morning, the school finished in the early afternoon. This would allow him, after returning home for a siesta, to spend the later part of the evening working on his novel.

At first, whenever he had come to Nicosia, he had left Sappho with my wife at our colonial bungalow where she played with our youngest son who was almost the same age as she was. Finding her a delightful child and remarkably well-behaved, Leonora became very fond of her. But once Larry started work at the Gymnasium it was no longer practical for him to bring her up from Kyrenia every day, so he took on an elderly Greek woman to look after her. She proved to be a kind and conscientious nurse with whom Sappho was content to be left while Larry was away.

Although he was working in the evenings not only on his novel but on articles for *Punch* on the more comic aspects of diplomatic life as he had experienced it in Belgrade, he found time to make friends among the more amusing, if not the most respectable, of the English who had settled or were on holiday in Kyrenia. Most of the town's British inhabitants were former colonial servants who had chosen Cyprus, and particularly Kyrenia, for their retirement because of its agreeable climate and the attraction of being able to live far more comfortably on their pensions than would have been possible had they returned to England. The arrival of a young Englishman, wifeless, but with a small child, and so impecunious that he could only afford cheap lodging in a Cypriot house was scandal enough, but that he should have accepted to teach at the Pan-Cyprian Gymnasium, a known hotbed of anti-British propaganda, and should have chosen some of his least desirable compatriots as his friends, put him beyond the pale.

This did not worry Larry. He was always discriminating in his friendships, sometimes oddly so, but it was certainly not among retired colonial officials that he was likely to find the kind of companionship he enjoyed. According to rumour reaching us in Nicosia, enjoy himself he certainly did when he abandoned his novel for an evening out in chosen company at his favourite bar. Although still far from affluent, a fairly dedicated drinker himself, he was always extremely generous, whenever he had money, in buying drinks for his friends. These parties, of which he was largely the instigator and which his talk did so much to animate, became notorious among the strait-laced British for their occasional disorderliness and the late hours at which they broke up.

Fortunately for us, at least once a week when he had finished at the Gymnasium he would call at our house for a drink before returning to Kyrenia. He could easily be persuaded to stay on to dinner and it was often midnight before he left. While we had made a number of close Cypriot and British friends, they tended to be rather sober and serious-minded. To our relief evenings with Larry were neither. The foibles of his colleagues and singular behaviour and attitudes of his pupils at the Gymnasium provided him with a source of highly amusing stories, as did, later, his vicissitudes when buying and restoring his cottage in Bellapaix.

When he was very young, before settling to become a writer, he had started on a career as a jazz pianist playing in bars and nightclubs. At one time when we were lucky enough to have a piano in the house, he would play and Leonora would join him in singing blues from their considerable repertoire.

Although he drank a good deal, he was not always, as we discovered, dependent on alcohol to be at his most entertaining. He had apparently been drinking rather more heavily than usual when, after an hilarious impersonation which had left him crawling around on the floor, he was so unsteady that I had to help him to his feet. It was only after he had left that we found that the Gordon's gin bottle, which he had almost emptied, had been filled by our servant with filtered water.

It was not always to spend the evening at our house that he lingered on after work instead of returning to Kyrenia. Like his stories about the Gymnasium, those he gathered from his excursions into the brothels of Nicosia, apart from their humour, were often revealing of Cypriot character and mores at the time. A satisfied young man he encountered in one of them assured him that with the influx of girls attracted by the British Army, life was much healthier in the towns, but that there was still far too much masturbation in the villages. A girl from Athens to whom he commented on a practice then much favoured by the mainland Greeks as providing the maximum of pleasure with minimal risk of undesirable complications responded with a giggle that it had never been asked of her since she had come to Cyprus. 'There's only one thing they think of doing here and they do it so often that they soon wear themselves out.'

About the time Larry started on his cottage at Bellapaix, Marie Millington-Drake arrived in Kyrenia with the intention of building a house on a plot of land close to the sea. She was an intelligent and extremely attractive girl who was engaged, or approximately so, to an Austrian prince of a famously rich and aristocratic family. Although her good looks alone would have assured her of Larry's attention, he must have found her prospective grand marriage added to her glamour for he frequently referred to it when talking about her. On learning of her plan to build a house, he advised her to have it designed by Austin Harrison, an English architect of great charm and distinction who lived in a village near

Kyrenia. Austin accepted the commission. Preoccupied with the affair of Marie's house, as well as his own, Larry became less inclined to linger after school hours in Nicosia.

Once the Bellapaix house was finished, he asked his mother to come out to look after Sappho. She was a convivial Irish woman, devoted to her granddaughter at sight and quickly gaining her affection. She adapted easily, even gaily, to life at Bellapaix, fortified by endless cigarettes and gentle gin tippling towards evening.

Larry had shown considerable taste in what he had made of a rather ordinary peasant's cottage. Simply decorated and furnished, its rooms were cool and light, their white walls enlivened by his own Matisse-inspired drawings. Its most attractive feature was the terrace, on to which most of the rooms opened, with its splendid view over the olive woods to Kyrenia and the sea. It was here that, generous as ever, he entertained his friends to parties which often ended with a moonlit visit to the abbey ruins nearby.

Work on Marie's house had begun but when she invited us to a picnic to see how it was progressing, the building was only a shell and it was difficult to imagine how it was going to turn out. I do not know if it was ever completed. The political situation was becoming daily more precarious. It was not long after the picnic that both Marie and Austin decided to leave the island.

There were to be changes in Larry's life, too. It was obvious that he could not go on teaching at the Gymnasium much longer. When the post of government information officer became vacant, I suggested to the Governor that Larry's fluent Greek, phil-Hellene background and experience in the Belgrade embassy made him an ideal candidate. The Governor agreed and Larry was offered and accepted the job. In some respects his appointment was a success as he got on well with the ever increasing hordes of visiting journalists, but, as I should have foreseen, the Greek Cypriots, who had welcomed him as a teacher at the Gymnasium, looked on his transfer to the colonial government with considerable suspicion.

Before he had taken up his new appointment, the psychoanalyst to whom he had sent Eve for treatment in England declared himself satisfied that she was cured. She wrote to Larry to say that she was coming out to join him. On her return, she seemed to be fully recovered, but there was inevitably tension between her and old Mrs Durrell. This had an unsettling effect on poor Sappho. To give mother and daughter a better chance of restoring their fractured relationship than in the fraught atmosphere at Bellapaix, Leonora invited them to stay for a week in the cottage we rented by the then unspoilt beach to the south of Famagusta. The visit was a success in bringing them emotionally close again. By the time they left there was no doubt of their mutual happiness at being reunited.

Leonora had enjoyed Eve's company but it had quickly become clear to her that however effective analysis had been in dealing with the problem of her breakdown, it had not reconciled her to settling back to life with Larry. Whenever she spoke of him it was with extreme bitterness.

Drawing on Paddy's account of his visit to the Durrells in Rhodes, I used to tease Leonora, long before she met either of them, by citing, as an example to be followed, the behaviour of this glamorous beauty from Alexandria who, when not cooking delicious meals for her husband, was content to sit at his feet in silent adoration while he talked. Now, as Eve revealed her inward rage at always being left out of the conversation and at the habit Larry's friends had of strolling into the kitchen to savour the appetizing smell of the food she was preparing, without ever offering to help, Leonora, while sympathizing with her, was amused to learn how widely my portrayal of her had missed the mark.

Her complaints about Larry were endless, but what had riled her most and to which she attributed her breakdown, was his obsession with psychoanalysing her. He had been attracted to the writings of a variety of esoteric teachers from Mila Repa, the Tibetan Buddhist saint, to such questionable gurus as Gurdjieff and Ouspensky, but it was by his delving into the works of Freud that he had been most profoundly influenced. With no other victim available, it was to his wife that he had turned to experiment with his own version of Freudian analysis. Ruthlessly, so she claimed, he had interpreted her every word and action as the consequences of her relationship with one or other of her parents or the subconscious reflex to some buried horror in her childhood or adolescence. This ended by so fraying her nerves that, with the strain of travel, she had lost control and become, as Larry himself had described her condition, 'violently schizophrenic'.

On her return to Bellapaix rumour reached us in Nicosia that all was not well between them. Evidence of how disastrously their relationship had developed was dramatically revealed at a morning reception for journalists at Government House. Officials invited to attend were expected to arrive early, but while the rest of us turned up dutifully on time the information officer who had been responsible for sending out the invitations was still missing when the guests began to arrive. It was not Larry but Eve who appeared first, her beauty marred by a very black eye. When asked what had happened, she hissed ferociously, 'Larry! – But wait till you see *him*!'

When he arrived, although it was extremely hot, he was muffled in a silk scarf. He had tucked it high under his chin, but it failed to hide altogether the lacerations on his neck from what must have been a tigerish clawing. Ironically, according to Larry, the fracas had been caused by Eve's tenacity in sticking to the edict of his pet psychoanalyst who had laid down that if she was to return to her husband it should be in the strictly limited role of housekeeper and mother of their child. Shortly afterwards, Eve left the island to return to London, taking Sappho with her.

Larry's first wife, by whom he also had had a daughter, had left him some years before. This second desertion, whatever its emotional import, he took as a blow to his self-esteem. Determined to prove that it was not as a lover that he had failed, he set himself to a wild campaign of seductions aimed at conquests not too easily to be obtained and desirable enough to repair the damage to his ego. But the scope was limited. With the increasing violence, many of the female expatriates had left. Those who remained were mostly the loyal wives of government officials or businessmen whose interests detained them from leaving. For a month or two Larry's campaign created near panic. Wives were packed off to England or bustled away by husbands who abruptly found they had no reason to stay on. This domestic flutter subsided as suddenly as it had begun (unlike the exploding bombs and bullets aimed at the British which daily became more numerous) with the entry into Larry's life of another Alexandrian beauty, this time blonde and with a French rather than English background.

Claude was the opposite of Eve not only in the colour of her hair but her personality as well. With intellectual pretensions and literary ambitions of her own, there was no question of her staying silent while Larry talked. He had by now moved into a house in Nicosia which he shared with the Governor's ADC. In spite of his other preoccupations, until Claude became such a consuming one, we saw more of him than at any time since his arrival. We had recently moved from the colonial bungalow to an old Turkish house just outside the town's medieval walls. Situated in the neutral Armenian quarter, it was generally out of bounds to terrorist activities. Among its many attractions was a courtyard centred on a large goldfish tank covered with water lilies and surrounded by clumps of papyrus and pots of sub-tropical flowers. As curfews became more frequent, we were able to enjoy its cool seclusion instead of being shut up indoors like most of the population. Larry, as a government official, was unrestricted in his movements. Whether there was a curfew or not, he would come to lunch or dinner two or three times a week. Inevitably, we discussed the political situation, but – as he was to write in *Bitter Lemons* – 'we tempered the preoccupations which grew out of it with the more congenial gossip about common friends and the books – the endless books – with which we passed our inmost time'.

Sadly, though it may be a truth ungenerous to recall, when Claude was present on such occasions, it was difficult not to regret the unfortunate Eve's reluctant silences.

Larry had chosen to come to Cyprus to write a novel. Although prone to an irregular way of life and forced to teach and take a government post instead of living on his savings, he had remained throughout his stay dedicated to his original intention. Now, on one of his visits to our house, he announced triumphantly that the novel was finished and left us with the manuscript of *Justine* to read.

No author wishes for anything but unstinted praise from the recipient of a manuscript of his as yet unpublished work. Happily, we found plenty to applaud in its highly entertaining comedy and splendidly evocative set pieces, but I did tentatively suggest that here and there he might have allowed the writing to become a trifle over-lush. 'Oh yes,' he said, 'there's still a lot of work to be done on it. I have asked for galley proofs so as to make corrections more easily. In any case Faber always make me rewrite everything I send them. They gave *The Marine Venus* (a book he had recently written about Rhodes) to one of their poets who took whole chunks out of it.'

Weeks later, even more triumphant than on his earlier visit, he announced that Faber were delighted with the book and did not want a word of it changed.

Bombs and bullets had by this time made life on the island so hazardous that we decided that Leonora with our youngest child, who had stayed on with us, should return to England. After they left, I often used to call at Larry's house for a drink in the evenings. As a government official, he was fair game for the assassin's bullet. Wisely, he had taken precautions, but it was a startling experience, until one got used to it, to be confronted, when in response to the bell the door was flung open, by Larry – in the hot weather as often as not stark naked – armed with a 12-bore double-barrelled shotgun pointed at close range at one's chest. In contrast to this fearsome weapon, in length not far short of his own height, he carried for daytime protection a minute pearl-handled pistol stuffed into his breast pocket with the butt sticking out. Fortunately he never had to use either weapon in self-defence. But now a drama of a quite different kind loomed for him, not from within the island but from some remote naval station east of Suez.

From the start Larry and Claude had carried on their liaison without the smallest attempt at discretion. Indeed, with such abandon that after the first impact gossips were left with nothing to gossip about. That Claude was married was not in doubt as she had two children at school in Nicosia. As she never mentioned her husband, it was assumed that, if not divorced, she was at least formally separated from him. Suddenly, outside all expectation, a cable arrived to announce that, posted back to England, he had contrived a stopover in Cyprus to see his family.

Claude and Larry panicked. It would have been impossible for them to deny that their relationship was close since the children had seen them so frequently together. To make all seem innocent, they decided that Claude should tell her husband that Larry and Richard (the ADC with whom Larry shared the house) were homosexuals and that she and Larry were no more than the best of friends. Either because they thought it unnecessary or feared he might not acquiesce, they did not tell Richard of what they had planned. Over-confident, they arranged a dinner party for the five of them. All went well until at the very end when, according to the account Larry gave me, as the party was breaking up, the husband in a genial aside to Richard said something to the effect of what nice chaps they were and what a lot of fun they must have together.

Richard's outraged retort was too obviously genuine not to be believed. With the truth revealed, the sailor's reaction was unexpected. As genial as ever, he simply sailed away, quite happy, it seemed, to leave not only Claude but the two children to Larry's charge.

Now my own time in Cyprus was coming to an end. On the evening before my flight home I invited Larry and Claude to dinner. As usual we dined in the courtyard. With high summer coming on it was hot outside but the water tank and a light breeze from the Kyrenia hills kept the courtyard cool. Our old cook, Mirem, knowing that this would be the last meal she would prepare for me, produced the best of her Turkish dishes. It was an enjoyable evening and a remarkably peaceful one. Not a single shot was fired and not a bomb exploded. The meal over, we sat on drinking, Larry and Claude facing each other across the table, I at one end between them. The talk turned to my impending departure. Claude said how lucky I was to be going back as London was her favourite city. The bitterness of Larry's love–hatred for Britain and anything British was immediately aroused.

'What do you find so wonderful about London?'

'Apart from anything else it's the only city I know where a girl can go into a bar by herself without getting her bottom pinched.'

'Christ! I suppose you're the sort of woman who, if anyone pinches her bottom, calls out the flying squad!'

I forget Claude's response but it enraged Larry even more. They went on shouting at each other across the table until Larry suddenly pulled the pistol out of his breast pocket and started firing it over her head into the wall behind her. Several of the houses close by had been taken over by British Army officers. At the sound of shots, windows were flung open and there was a cry of 'Call out the guard!' In minutes, an armoured car drew up outside and soldiers started banging at the door. I went out and spoke to them. Denying I had heard any shots, I managed to persuade them that it was a false alarm.

By now Larry and Claude had calmed down. They left soon afterwards. I went out into the garden with them to say goodbye. It was the last time I was to see Claude. She and Larry were married soon after leaving Cyprus. A few years later she died in hospital in Switzerland. It was fifteen years before I saw Larry again.

Faber had been right. *Justine*, published without a word being changed, was praised by the critics and, unlike any of his previous books, became a best-seller. I wrote to congratulate him but he did not reply. I might have thought he had been piqued by my mild criticism had I not heard at the same time of old friends who had tried to visit him at his new home in Provence but had been turned away. Others who had written to him had received uncharacteristically off-hand or arrogant replies. John Lehmann, who had published Durrell's poems in the *London Magazine*, was incensed at being sent, in response to a letter of his own, an unsigned letter typed on the back of a proof copy of an ecstatic French review of his books.

I would never have imagined that Larry would be affected by success as he appeared to have been. If he had changed, I thought it might be due to the influence of Claude and her pretensions. Certainly with the completion of *The Alexandria Quartet* he became, not only successful, but famous and rich.

Ten years later I had a postcard from him announcing the production of his play *An Irish Faust* at a theatre in Hamburg. I was surprised that after such a long silence he had thought of sending it to me or bothered to find out my address. There was no possibility of my going to Hamburg to see the play.

Five years on in London I had lunch with Wallace Southam, an old friend from our time in Athens. When I told him that I was about to spend a month in Montpellier, he suggested that I should call on Larry who was living only a few miles away at Sommières. On retiring from business, Wallace had become the fund-raiser for a hospice for the dying. He had written to Larry asking for permission to produce a record of his poems to be sold on behalf of the hospice. Larry had generously agreed.

Not long afterwards he had invited Wallace to stay at

Sommières. He had written the book of a musical and wanted Wallace, who was a gifted composer, to set the lyrics to music. The visit was not a success. Wallace thought nothing of the lyrics and was amazed to find Larry so self-deceiving as to be satisfied with them. He was shocked by how much he was drinking and his relations with his housekeeper whom he described as a 'drunken harridan'. He gave me his telephone number but after what he had said, I doubted whether I would use it. Once in Montpellier, I became curious and, recalling how much I had enjoyed his company in the past, though apprehensive, I rang him up. I need not have worried. He declared himself delighted to have the chance of seeing me again and invited me to lunch the next day. I should come early so that we could talk.

I had no difficulty in finding the house but could hardly believe that it was his. At a time when there were so many attractive houses to be bought in Provence, he had settled for a Charles Addams monster, surrounded by tall, gloomy trees, standing on its own about half a mile from the town. He opened the door himself and gave me a warm welcome. I was struck by how much his appearance had changed. His features had become coarser and curiously lumpy. His head seemed even larger than before in proportion to his body. He led me through into the drawing-room. It was long and dark, its only light coming from a kind of conservatory at one end. We sat on a sofa facing into it. There was a table in front of us with glasses and half a bottle of red wine.

I told him how sorry I had been to hear belatedly of Claude's death. 'Oh yes,' he said, so casually that I wondered how the marriage might have turned out. 'She died in Switzerland.' I asked after Sappho. She had been a beautiful child, I imagined she must be strikingly good-looking now she had grown up. No, she wasn't particularly good-looking. His tone was coolly disparaging. 'She comes to stay sometimes. The trouble about my family is that they're all after my money.'

We talked about Cyprus and the friends we had made there. I thought he might have asked after Leonora who had entertained him so frequently, but he ignored any mention I made of her in the conversation. The bottle on the table was quickly finished. While he went to fetch another, I turned to look round the room. I was astonished at its ugliness. It was filled with fussy, semi-antique furniture. Some gilded bronze statuettes on a table did nothing to dispel the gloom. Remembering the airy lightness of his cottage in Bellapaix, I could not believe that this dreary clutter was of his own choosing. When he came back with the wine, I asked him if he had taken the house furnished. No: everything in it, he assured me, had been bought by Claude and himself.

The wine finished, it was time for lunch. He explained that we would have to go to a restaurant in Sommières as his cook/housekeeper had fallen into the empty swimming-pool and broken her leg. She was, I supposed, the drunken harridan of whom Wallace had spoken. At the restaurant he was greeted as a valued patron. We had an excellent meal. Most of the talk was about his books. He was bitter that while in other countries they had continued to receive excellent reviews, after their early enthusiasm the English critics had become hostile. This, he believed, was because, academics themselves, they were reluctant to admit the merits of a writer who had not been to a university. When I regretted that he had written so little poetry in recent years, he said that he had been too taken up with his novels. He asked me if I had read any of them. I had to confess that I had only read one. Compared to *The Alexandria Quartet*, I had found the writing inventive rather than creative. He accepted this, but said that he was about to start on a new novel of which he had high expectations. It arose out of his research into the history of the Knights Templar in Languedoc. After lunch when the bill arrived, he brought out of his wallet a note of an impressively high denomination, remarking that he did not expect that I had seen one like it often. I readily confessed that I hadn't.

Before I left he asked me to go out to Sunday lunch with him to friends who had a ranch in the Camargue. I was to call for him at nine o'clock. When I arrived he had already got through his first bottle of red wine. We drank the best part of another before starting out. He told me the ranch was owned by the daughter of Richard Aldington, the writer, who had died a few years before. He and Larry, both disgruntled with their treatment by English critics, had become close friends. We lunched surrounded by horses. The other guests were old Camargue hands. From what he told me, Aldington had had near-fascist views. It seemed he might have been influenced by them himself, for he had moved far to the right. On the way back he tried to convince me that Wilson, who was then prime minister, was planning to hand Britain over to the Russians.

On subsequent visits I invited him to lunch with me in Montpellier but he insisted on my going to Sommières. There were times when we talked as enjoyably as in the past, but I found his continual drinking and the gloom of the house profoundly depressing. He appeared obsessed with promoting his own publicity and tried to persuade me to take part in a French radio programme about him, until I pointed out that the audience would not be faintly interested in the views of someone so totally unknown to them. The alleged rapaciousness of his family and his bitterness against England and the English were never left out of the conversation for long. The roots of the latter were incidentally revealed when, recalling how he had used to quote from Mila Repa, I told him of my own interest in Tibetan Buddhism which, with Tibet forbidden to travellers at the time, had taken me on a journey to visit the Tibetan community in Darjeeling. I had reached the town by the little, toy-like, rack-and-pinion railway which winds up from the plains through the tea plantations, in the Himalayan foothills. The town had been full of emotive relics of the Raj, including a school where boys still wore English-type uniforms, and a faded hotel complete with *thés dansants* and Palm Court orchestra.

Larry listened with interest. I knew vaguely that he had an Anglo-Indian background, but I had never head him speak of it. Now he told me that it was in Darjeeling that he had been brought up. His father had been the engineer in charge of the little railway on which I had travelled. As a child he had been educated at the school I had remarked on and had worn its uniform. When he was twelve, his parents had sent him away to a minor public school in England. Ignorant of English schoolboy practices and conventions, undersized and with a chi-chi accent, he had been mercilessly tormented. It had turned him against England for good though, curiously, not against all products of the public school system. Among his wilder generalizations, and one which he often repeated, was his contention that the only Englishmen worth knowing were old Etonians.

In spite of his success, he seemed lonely and far from happy.

Apart from the people I had met in the Camargue and Xan Fielding whom he had known in Greece but who lived some distance away, he did not mention having any friends in the neighbourhood. On my last visit he had with him a tedious literary gentleman from Montpellier whose company I could only suppose he tolerated because he was dedicated to promoting his books on French radio and television. We left the house together. I asked him how long Larry had been drinking so much. He assured me that recently he had cut down a lot. Before, it had been gin all day long. Since his doctor had told him he was going to kill himself, he had given up spirits and drank only wine. I mentioned how lonely he seemed to be. 'Oh no, he's always giving interviews to the press, and film crews frequently come to make documentaries about him.'

We had made a vague arrangement that I should go to see him again before I left Montpellier, but I felt, and he may well have felt the same, that we had little more to say to each other. When I rang him up before leaving he told me that he was about to fly to some town in northern France where the students were putting on one of his plays. We agreed that we must meet in Paris where I would shortly be working. I had not been settled there long when a young theatrical producer came to see me with a letter from Larry asking me if I could arrange a subsidy for the production of one of his plays in a suburban theatre. I had to explain that I had no money available for any such purpose. Sometime afterwards I came on Larry by chance in the Dôme. His reception was cool. It was our last meeting. He had not forgiven me for my failure to help in putting on his play.

[4]

Graham Sebastian
Our Man in Milan

When I first arrived in Milan early in 1948 it was still winter. The city had been bombed during the war and was still being rebuilt. The opera house and Galleria had been restored but there were grim chasms in the streets near the centre. Most of the buildings which remained intact were scarred and shabby. From the hub of the cathedral square drab thoroughfares along which trams screeched and groaned spread their tentacles into the hideous industrial agglomeration which surrounded the city. Smoke from factory chimneys rose straight into the still air to merge into a grey ceiling of closely packed cloud.

I had come out alone, I knew no one and, after Athens, I found the climate and atmosphere depressing. I was unsuccessful in my search for somewhere to live for there were few flats or houses to let and those I saw were unsuitable. In London the Italian owner of a villa twelve miles out in the Brianza had suggested we might take part of it. We could have a wing to ourselves, her servants would look after us and we could pay whatever we could afford towards its upkeep. At a half-hour drive from the centre it sounded impractical, but I decided I might, at least, have a look at it.

When I set out the usual murk hung over the city. In the open plain it thickened to a dense fog. Warned of my visit the lodge-keeper came out to open the villa gates for me. The road had been flat all the way but the drive beyond the gates rose steeply between an avenue of tall trees. As the fog thinned to a white mist, I could see the moisture dripping from their branches. Then as the drive levelled out, the mist parted and I was dazzled by brilliant sunlight flooding down from a blue sky. The house stood back at the top of the slope, a classical eighteenth-century villa with stucco walls and tiled roof. Two wings jutting out in front were connected by a colonnade to form a courtyard. In the middle of it a fountain threw up a single jet which fell back into a stone basin. I drove round it and stopped under the portico which sheltered the front door.

At the sound of my car the administrator appeared accompanied by the butler. He offered to show me round the part of the house we could occupy. Amelio, the butler, unlocked the door and folded back the shutters. I followed the administrator into the hall which ran the full width of the house. It had glass-panelled doors at the opposite end which opened on to a broad terrace. The view from it was framed by cedars and redwoods planted on either side of the park which sloped down to a wooded valley. In the middle distance a plateau, its fields edged with mulberries, receded to the mountains around Lake Como above which, detached from them by a blue haze and deeply snow covered, the entire range of the Alps from Monte Rosa to the Bergamasco peaks lay gleaming under the clear sky.

Back in the house the administrator guided me up a broad staircase to one side of the hall. A cardinal's hat with immense tassels floated above the well on a cord suspended from the ceiling. We turned off along a corridor which led to a drawing-room overlooking a second courtyard and beyond it to three bedrooms all handsomely furnished and with views towards the Alps. Along another corridor leading to an orangerie were some smaller bedrooms suitable for the children.

My mind had been made up from the moment I had driven out of the fog into the sunlight. Our tour concluded I told the administrator that we would like to move in as soon as possible. He suggested that we should wait until the weather was warmer and the central heating no longer necessary. When he told me what it would cost, I agreed to put off our arrival until the spring.

Two months later I drove out to Gernetto on a warm sunny evening in early April. Leonora and the children arrived the next day. The children were the first explorers. They vanished into the garden to return after an hour chattering of a Swiss chalet in the park, a grotto into which the unwary could be lured and doused with water, a penny-farthing in the stables, a coach and a horse called Sigefreda. When asked how they managed to discover so much so quickly they replied that the gardener's children had shown them round. 'Did they speak English?' 'No, we just talked and they understood.' 'Did you understand them?' 'Of course!'

At the weekend we did our own exploring. We started with the great shuttered rooms in the old part of the house, the large and smaller drawing-rooms, the picture gallery and the chapel with a marble by Canova. Upstairs we came first to the library which like the hall beneath it stretched the full width of the house with windows at each end. Beyond it the state bedroom boasted an enormous gilded bed ruminated upon by the melancholy eyes of farm and domestic animals depicted in huge paintings on the walls. There were scores of lesser rooms of all shapes and sizes, bedrooms, their hangings fusty with age, bathrooms with tubs encased in mahogany and lavatories like thrones, a museum of minerals, a cabinet of old master drawings, sitting rooms and dressing-rooms, these last surrounded by enough cupboards to have housed the clothes of a dozen families with wardrobes as modest as our own.

Exploration of the park and grounds was as enjoyable if less rich in the unexpected. An arboretum contained rare specimens, their names unknown to us until identified by Bertie Moore when he came to stay. The avenue which lined the drive was of tulip trees which burst into clouds of pale green cup-like blooms. The woods were full of wild flowers, violets, primroses, anemones and lilies-of-the-valley, these last growing in such profusion that their scent carried to our bedroom windows. There were wild strawberries, too, of which we picked basketfuls on Sunday mornings to take back for lunch.

Soon it became warm enough to sit out on the terrace after dinner. One evening a full moon and the nightingales singing in the woods kept us up later than usual. Hearing a noise behind us we turned to see a troop of elderly peasants shuffling in single file across the hall. Each had a blanket round his shoulders, a lantern in one hand and an ancient gun in the other. In the morning Amelio explained they were the villa guards who were posted at night in the ground-floor rooms to protect the house against bandits.

We stayed through the summer and autumn but in winter, enchanting as the grounds appeared under a Christmas snowfall, the cold became intolerable. We crouched round the open fire in the drawing room but when we left it we froze. The ducts of the central heating emitted through their grills more smoke than heat. We learned that their ramifications had a life of their own when we encountered a rat and a scorpion which had come up through a broken grill in our bathroom.

Although our first heating bill made us waver it was illness which finally drove us out. We returned again in the spring, but in the autumn we moved into a flat in the city.

Our move coincided with the arrival of our new consul-general, Graham Sebastian. At a glance you might have taken him for a bit of an old buffer with his short-cut hair brushed back, features ruddily handsome, an eye-glass screwed in over one Nordic blue eye as (had you made an early call at the office) he pondered his copy of *The Times*. Conventionally British in turn-out – old college or regimental tie, white shirt freshly laundered, well tailored suit of a discreet check, sturdy brogues with toe caps handsomely polished – you could have taken him for a likely denizen of the pavilion at Lord's or a near-permanent fixture at the Oxford and Cambridge or United Services Club.

Had you delayed your call until an hour or so later you might have got quite a different impression on finding him, newspaper folded away and files dispatched, with his head bent over a work of the finest petit-point as he copied without a line drawn on the canvas but with stitches meticulously counted a design taken from some rich fabric in a Florentine painting or embroidery on a Byzantine cope. He might have surprised you, too, when, your presence announced, he took not the slightest notice until approaching close to his desk you finally drew his attention. Once drawn, dropping his canvas he would have reached across his desk for the switch on a little black box which was attached by a wire to a plug in his ear. By now you would have realized that without the box turned on he was all but stone deaf. This infirmity had been brought about by a shell burst splitting his eardrums during the fighting in Salonica in the First World War; though not before he had been awarded the D.S.O. for gallantry in action.

In his youth Graham had done himself out of his chosen career in the Foreign Office by over-indulgence in theatricals to the detriment of his studies while at Oxford. After failing in the higher exam he had been accepted for the Consular Service, then an organization on its own, less prestigious and less well paid than the Diplomatic.

His career had taken him across Asia and Europe from China to Belgium by way of Thailand, Romania, Greece and Sweden. Now in his late fifties he had been appointed to Milan as his final posting. The possessions he had brought with him included trophies from all the countries in which he had worked: rock crystal and jade from China, a Buddha head in the Khmer style from Bangkok and embroidery from Romania where, encouraged by Queen Marie, he had first taken to needle and canvas, a hobby which was to engage him increasingly on his retirement to England where his work was soon acknowledged as equal to the finest in the country.

But Greece had been his great love. His library contained a comprehensive collection of books on its history in the Byzantine and Frankish periods while the shelves were topped by an impressive array of ancient Greek helmets. A rare archaic bronze athlete had a pedestal to itself. Two large Edward Lear watercolours, bought long before his paintings became sought after by collectors, romantically evoked the landscapes of Corfu and the Epirus.

When the Germans invaded Greece in 1941, as consul in the Piraeus, keeping the coolest of heads, he had successfully organized the evacuation of a horde of panicky British subjects from Athens to Egypt. On arrival in Cairo he had been appointed an adviser on Greek affairs.

His disagreement with what he believed, justifiably as it proved, to be the Foreign Office's over-emphasis on the future importance of the royal family in the politics of post-war, liberated Greece resulted in his transfer to neutral Sweden as consul in Bergen.

From Sweden (he had Swedish ancestry himself) he had brought with him among his treasures fine glass and china. And from Belgium, where stationed in Antwerp he had been oblivious of the flying bombs which sent his staff scuttling for cover, he had enticed to accompany him to Milan an exceptionally ugly but highly accomplished Luxembourgeoise cook.

Our move to a flat in the city, close to the consulate above which

Graham lived, had the fortunate consequence that we got to know him and appreciate his many remarkable qualities more quickly that we might have done had we stayed on at Gernetto. Certainly without his friendship our lives would have been greatly impoverished, for we owed much to his generous hospitality, wise advice and readiness to let us draw on his profound knowledge covering a wide range of subjects.

His passion for the theatre and Shakespeare in particular had not diminished since his Oxford days. He had known many of the leading actors and actresses of the period including Sybil Thorndyke and her husband, Hugh Casson. Ralph Richardson had been a friend from early in his acting career. Having seen Henry Irving as a child and, later, Sarah Bernhardt and the Duse on the stage, he was disinclined to believe that the theatre in Milan had anything worthwhile to offer. I failed to persuade him to go to any of the young Georgio Strehler's productions at the Teatro Piccolo, but, when invited to *Richard III* at another theatre, he felt obliged to accept and asked me to go with him. The evening proved an ordeal. The play did not begin until an hour after the advertised time and was so dragged out that it was long after midnight when the cry 'my kingdom for a horse' rang out unheard by Graham, who had long since switched off his black box and shamelessly sunk into sleep.

If the Milanese theatre failed him he found plenty of scope for pursuing some of his other interests. His preference in architecture was for the Romanesque of which there were many fine examples in the region. He made a collection of photographs of the lions supporting the columns at the entrances to the great churches of the period in the Lombardy plain. At weekends he took us to see some of the smaller and lesser-known examples of the Romanesque which he had discovered, among them a little circular church in the middle of a field and another deep in a forest with frescos so early they appeared almost Pompeian. His favourite outing was to the little town of Castiglione Olona which had a church in the style of Bruneleschi and frescos by Massolino in the collegiate chapel. On the hill above the town he had found a tavern which sold an excellent rough country wine with which they served a coarse, homemade bread and *vecchio grana*, the matured version of Parmesan cheese.

He was very knowledgeable on Italian painting especially the works of the early Siennese and Florentine masters. Visiting frescoed churches with him was always instructive but could be embarrassing. In some people deafness reduces their speech to a low mumble, while in others it makes them talk much louder that they realize. Graham belonged to the second category. Once embarked on a disquisition, his voice booming back from rounded apse or vaulted roof, it was impossible to stop him even when Mass was in progress and priest and congregation tried to hush him into silence.

At some stage in his career he had become a close friend of Bernard Berenson, the great art historian whose attributions had been relied upon by American collectors at the turn of the century. When he came to Milan on a visit, Graham asked him and his secretary/companion, Nicky Mariano, to dinner. He also invited Professor Dellacqua, the director of the Brera, and his wife, and myself, on my own as Leonora was in England. On the evening of the dinner the Dellacquas dropped out at the last moment, so that there were only four of us at the dinner table. Berenson, who was already well into his eighties, was frail but as intellectually alert as ever though his voice had become weak. When he tried to talk to Graham even with the help of the little black box he failed to get through to him. After several attempts he turned to me dryly remarking that he supposed we would have to talk.

His evident conjecture that I was unlikely to be worth talking to was unnerving as I had heard that he could be abrasive if he judged that the company he was with did not come up to his high intellectual standards. Playing safe I told him of our expeditions with Graham in search of the Romanesque. He asked me if we had been to Borgo San Donino. I told him that it was one of the churches Graham had taken us to and remarked, stealing the phrase from Proust, that a relief on its exterior was 'almost Persian'. Whether or not he recognised the Proustian theft he agreed that there were often touches of the oriental in the Italian Romanesque.

Playing still safer I lured him into reminiscence and was rewarded with, among other scenes from his past, an account of Milan as he had first known it, when the aristocracy, the women all jewels and plumed hats, paraded in their coaches every evening up and down the Via Monte Napoleone. At the Scala the boxes were privately owned by the leading families, but their occupants rarely sat through the whole of an opera, preferring to show off their finery while gossiping in the foyer, and only returning to their seats when an attendant announced the imminent performance of a celebrated aria.

All this was lost to poor Graham, but fortunately Nicky Mariano's voice carried through to him so that the conversational impasse which had threatened when we first sat down at the table, was averted.

After the theatre Graham's great love was for music, especially opera. Having heard many of the most famous singers of the first half of the century in their most celebrated roles he so impressed the directors of the Scala with his knowledge and discernment that although the boxes were in much demand by Milanese notables, they agreed to let him have one in which, to our immense good luck, he offered us a share.

Living at Gernetto had restricted our visits to the opera as the performances never ended before midnight so that it was one o'clock or even later by the time we got back to the villa. We had tried to persuade Amelio and the lodge-keeper to give us keys so that we could let ourselves in, but, leaving us guilt-ridden, they politely declined explaining that they always stayed up for the *marchesa* no matter how late she returned.

Once we had moved into the city and had a share in Graham's box we went to the Scala once and sometimes twice a week throughout the season. The principal productions were superbly staged with all the leading singers of the time appearing in them, but while they could be heard in other opera houses throughout the world, it was the unrivalled brilliance of the chorus and orchestra, especially in the Italian repertoire which made the performances so uniquely remarkable. Highly conscious of their own pre-eminence they were collectively as temperamental as any of the individual prima donnas and gave just as much trouble to the management. For several weeks they had a feud with the state radio which, they claimed, paid too little for their relays. Every evening one of the double basses, an enormous man with a bald, egg-shaped head, strolled into the pit just as the opera was about to begin and armed with a pair of wirecutters snipped through the leads of the microphones along the front of the stage. They were generally contemptuous of conductors, believing they knew better themselves and scarcely giving them a glance during the performance. They had no liking for contemporary music. When I watched Stravinsky rehearsing a concert of his own works, they were so uncooperative that he was reduced to leaving the rostrum to remonstrate – too gently to be effective – with the more recalcitrant players.

Some months later I saw him avenged by Leonard Bernstein. When he walked into the theatre wearing a polo-neck sweater and looking even younger than he then was, their resistance stiffened. He started on Stravinsky's *Rite of Spring*. After the first few bars he stopped and asked the leader if they had ever played the piece before. On being told that they had many times, he retorted: 'Then you must have always played it wrong!'

After this exchange they realized that, despised American as he was and however youthful a prodigy, he was not going to let them get the better of him. When the leader announced that it was time to break for lunch, he refused to stop and kept them at it till they had performed the work to his satisfaction.

If Graham could sometimes be embarrassing when giving his views on works of art in churches where services were being conducted, he could also disconcert one at the opera when he appeared to be on the point of nodding off with the probability of letting out an outrageous snore. His appearance of somnolence was, however, deceptive, for at the end his comments would be so detailed and to the point that it was clear he had not missed a note throughout the performance.

In the foyer during the interval talking to his many Italian friends he would be outspoken in his criticisms which were often directed against the audience rather than the singers. 'The trouble with you Italians', he would announce, 'is that you're not really musical!' Such was his good humour that far from being offended they were highly amused to hear such a view expressed, especially by an Englishman, while some admitted that the frequent outbursts of unwarranted boos or applause justified his censure.

Shortly before he left Milan to start his retirement in England, Foreign Office inspectors criticized his tenure at the consulate for administrative shortcomings and lack of rapport with the British community. His attendance to administrative matters may have been perfunctory particularly if they interrupted him while at work on an exacting piece of embroidery. That he should have had little time for the business community was not surprising. They were certainly far too prosperous to need his support, nor was there much to attract him in their company, hard-headed philistines that they were and so bigoted that they boasted of never having had any Italians, apart from servants, in their houses. To British subjects in genuine difficulties, such as young travellers trapped by currency restrictions, for whom consular funds were not available, he was generous beyond his means in helping them out of his own resources.

What the inspectors could not mention in their report, since they knew nothing of it, was his personal popularity among the Milanese, including the high officials. This had done much to ease Anglo-Italian relations in the city at a time when they were under stress from such long-forgotten causes of discord as the Mogadishu incident and the extended occupation of Trieste by the British army.

We left for Cyprus in 1952 at about the same time as Graham started his retirement. After we had been on the island a few months he came to stay with us on his way to visit a retired ambassador in Egypt. He had already embarked in London on a Swedish ship bound for Famagusta when he heard that his ambassador friend had died of a heart attack. After Egypt he had planned to move to Izmir where David Balfour, whom he had known well when they were both in Greece before the war, was British consul. As Balfour was not expecting him for another month he asked, on arrival, if he could stay on with us. Fond as we were of him, this proved a trial as he was saving the batteries in his black box for Izmir and we were left hoarse from shouting in our efforts to get through to him. Otherwise he was the most amenable of guests content to spend hours reading up on the history of Cyprus or stitching away at his embroidery.

When he had first returned to England he had settled in with his brother and sister-in-law, but this had not proved a success. By the time we left Cyprus in 1956 when I was doomed to work for two years in London, he had moved into a basement flat in Bayswater on the edge of Notting Hill. This was the best he could afford on his meagre Foreign Office pension. The area was seedy, much of it taken over by Caribbeans, a still cheerful, smiling community though later to be soured when they became the victims of one of the earliest outbreaks of racist violence in London.

Returning from weekends in the country I had lunch with him most Mondays, bringing with me vegetables from our garden. The house in which he rented his flat was shabby, its walls peeling. From what one could glimpse through its windows his fellow tenants appeared far from prosperous. The area steps down to his front door looked uninviting, even treacherous. Before starting the descent the sound of grand opera blasting up from below was evidence of the occupier's taste in music being unusual for the neighbourhood. It was because he was always saving the batteries of his hearing aid that he had the volume of his record player turned up so high. This made it doubly difficult to attract his attention. Ringing the bell was useless. It was only after battering on the door and rapping as hard as I dared on the window that I managed to alert him to my arrival.

For a stranger entering the flat for the first time its interior must have been as unexpected as the fortissimo music he had heard when outside. In the restricted space of his living-room he had assembled all the treasures which he had displayed in his more spacious accommodation in Milan. Two walls were lined with bookcases topped by the ancient Greek helmets. The archaic bronze stood on its pedestal jammed in behind the sofa. He had reserved a place on his desk for the Khmer Buddha head. The Chinese rock-crystal rabbits were arranged on the shelf above the fireplace. The Edward Lears filled what remained of the space on the walls. Examples of his needlework abounded: a map of Greece in petit-point, curtains in cross-stitch, embroidered cushion covers and, perhaps, a half-finished kneeler for a Chelsea church abandoned when he had retired to the kitchen to cook lunch. His Luxembourgeoise cook, toad-like, bad-tempered and spitefully jealous of the charming Russian lady from Brussels who had regularly come to visit him in Milan, had produced memorable meals but all her best dishes had been prepared following Graham's instruction. Now in sole charge of his minute kitchen, painstaking with his pots and pans as with needle and canvas, the food he brought to the table after meticulous preparation, though simple – his Irish stew was a masterpiece – was always perfectly cooked. While his sitting-room, though inevitably dark from its situation, was not only welcomingly snug but rewarding to the eye because of its unusual contents, his bedroom which led out of it offered cold comfort. Poky and even darker with space for little more than his bed and a chest of drawers, it had sinister patches of damp spreading up the walls from the wainscoting.

Graham had always suffered from bronchitis. In Milan, after a particularly serious attack, his doctor had told me that he doubted if he had more than two years to live. Obviously a damp basement was likely to have a disastrous effect on his health. As soon as winter set in the bronchitis returned. Although his local doctor gave him medicine which checked it, if, as I descended the area steps for my Monday lunch, his record-player was silent, I was anxious about what state I might find him in as I battered on the door and waited for him to respond.

Fortunately he had a number of loyal friends who invited him to stay with them from time to time in the country. The most hospitable was Aubrey Moody, who had been a secretary at the embassy in Athens when Graham was consul in the Piraeus. After leaving the diplomatic service he had taken Holy Orders and become vicar of a parish in Essex. Graham was a frequent weekend guest at his rectory and always returned with his health improved.

Although he lost nothing of his genial manner and never complained of the insalubrious living conditions to which he had been reduced by his inadequate pension, I was pessimistic, with his Milanese doctor's foreboding in mind, about how long he could survive. On my last visit before we left London for Mexico City, he was suffering one of his worst attacks. When I said goodbye to him I feared that he might not last out until we were next in England. Should the damp basement prove fatal we would doubtless see his death announced in *The Times*. However saddening it would not have been unexpected, whereas the announcement about him which we eventually came upon one morning in the newspaper, so amazed us that we could hardly believe it to be true.

To the chagrin of his Luxembourgeoise cook, his charming

Russian friend from Brussels and, possibly, others in the past whose aspirations he had disappointed, he had always been the most obdurate of bachelors. That in his middle sixties, too impecunious to be a 'catch' and having hitherto stuck so firmly to the single life, he should have, as the announcement stated, married a Mrs Hilda Gardener of Coggeshall in Essex, a lady whose name he had never mentioned on my Monday visits, struck us as so unlikely that we hesitated before writing to congratulate him.

Back in England from Mexico we learned that he had met Hilda while a guest of Aubrey Moody, whose living was close to Coggeshall. Soon after our return they invited us to stay and we saw how miraculously changed for the better Graham's life had been by his marriage.

Hilda, who was one of the first women to have taken a degree at Girton, had many admirable qualities. She was intelligent, good company, broad-minded and, in pursuit of any cause she championed, tenacious and even formidable. Her first husband, an antiquarian bookseller, had come of an old-established Coggeshall brewing family. He had inherited the family property which had passed to Hilda on his death. The house was a wonderful old rambling place with a walled garden by the river, an archery ground and a grove of cricket-bat willows. To one side lay the maltings, no longer in use but an attractive jumble of rose-coloured brick; to the other, the stables, numerous outhouses and, an important bonus, a pub conveniently placed and part of the property. The house itself was full of fine old furniture and pictures, including a Constable sketch, an important Dutch seascape and a large painting of a country scene with horses by Moreland. It had a handsome library with a bow window overlooking the archery ground, a cosy buttery by the side entrance full of bottles and glasses, while below there were extensive, well-stocked cellars. Part of Hilda's book business was carried on in one of the outhouses. She also owned a bookshop in the nearby village of Kelveden.

With all this Graham had acquired a wife dedicated to looking after his health and well-being whose devotion he reciprocated, a delightful home with a roomy kitchen in which they could collaborate in producing delicious meals, along with such minor perks as cheap spirits from the pub and books at wholesale prices from the Kelveden shop.

To this welcome haven in which, like an old sea captain, he had come to settle after a lifetime of foreign travel, he had brought with him all the treasures he had acquired. The Greek helmets were ranged along the top of the library shelves on which space had been made for his books on medieval Greek history. The Edward Lears were hung in the drawing-room and the remainder were scattered about the house adding an exotic touch to the quantities of sober oak and mahogany.

He had, of course, brought his Foreign Office pension, too, but, more importantly, his tatting bag with its needles, thimbles, silks, wools and canvases. He had already been at work long enough to have produced an elaborately patterned waistcoat for Hilda (she was a stout lady so it must have required an enormous number of stitches), a handbag in petit-point and a set of table mats copied from illustrations in a medieval work on husbandry.

We invited them to stay whenever we were on holiday in England and exchanged visits almost every summer after my own retirement. Over the years they continued to collaborate happily in the kitchen and, before we sat down to the excellent food they had prepared, were as generous as ever with the drinks they served from the buttery and the wines they brought up from the cellar. While Hilda battled on at her good works, Graham was always stitching away at yet another of his needlework masterpieces. Sometimes he would be listening to music with the volume of his record-player turned up; at others he would be ready with his hearing aid switched on, to look up from his canvas and letting his monocle fall out of his eye, join in the conversation with an appropriate ancedote or a learned, bawdy or, at the mention of a Labour politician, caustic comment. If the conversation bored him he would switch off the little black box with an ostentatious sweep of his hand.

As inflation ate into Graham's pension and whatever financial resources Hilda's first husband had left her, the property which went with the old brewery shrank. The maltings was sold off to be converted into flats and the walled garden by the river went with it. Other outbuildings were sold or let. Gradually the more valuable objects in the house began to disappear. The Greek helmets vanished from the library and the rarer books from its shelves. The Khmer head and the archaic bronze were bought by the British Museum. The more important pictures were sent for auction at Sotheby's. Of the collection Graham had brought with him only the Edward Lears and the rock-crystal rabbits remained.

The loss of these possessions did not appear to diminish the good humour of either of them. Hilda saved now a neglected chapel and now a medieval tithe barn, while Graham kept on at his needlework until, with so much else gone, it came to nearly overwhelming the house as he turned out, not always shown to their best advantage and sometimes put to unsuitable use, an endless assortment of exquisitely embroidered curtains, carpets, rugs, cushion covers, screens, fire screens and, of course, waist-coats, skirts, jackets and handbags for Hilda.

When he reached his eighties his output began to flag a little but it was only a few weeks before he died that he let his eye-glass drop and abandoned needle and canvas for good.

Hilda lived on for some years after his death much revered for all that she had done for the village, her drawing-room frequented by a circle of devoted friends. But funds continued to run low. After she had reluctantly sold the Edward Lears all that was left of Graham's treasures were the Chinese rock-crystal rabbits on the drawing-room mantelpiece.

[5]
Peggy Guggenheim
an Exchange of Visits

Soon after we had settled at Gernetto I had to go to Venice to meet an embassy official. He invited me for drinks in the evening at the Ca'Dario which he was renting. Though not among the most imposing of the palaces on the Grand Canal it has a special appeal with its richly decorated façade and appearance of reaching far back into the city's past. Attracted by its exterior I had always wondered what it might be like inside.

Unfortunately I was delayed in leaving my hotel so that the sun had already set when the gondola I had hired nosed in alongside the Ca'Dario steps. These were partially submerged, the water needing to rise only a few inches to cover the paved entrance. My host greeted me from stairs which led to a more securely habitable level. It was already so dark that I could make out little of the interior as he guided me across an upper hall into the drawing room. This, too, was all shadowy gloom, its window giving only enough light to catch the gilding on the frame of a great mirror over the fireplace and those of some dim old masters on the walls.

He introduced me to his wife and their guests, two ladies sitting with their backs to the window on a settee. One, tall, slim and dark with hair sticking out as if recently rumpled, was Peggy Guggenheim, as notorious for the alleged number of her lovers as she was celebrated for her collection of contemporary art; the other, short, bundly and wearing, unfashionably for Venice, an elaborate hat, was Freya Stark, scarcely less famous for her finely written books and intrepid Arabian travels.

If I had been frustrated by the prevailing gloom from seeing as much as I would have liked of the interior of the palace, I was no less so at finding myself sitting opposite these two remarkable women without being able to get more than a vague idea of what they looked like since the only light came from the window behind them. Had I been able to see them more clearly I would have realised that Peggy's mouth only appeared so large because of the lipstick she kept jabbing on round it, while Freya's hat would have been accounted for by her need to hide the complete loss of hair on one side of her scalp.

I don't remember what was talked about but the conversation went easily enough. Pressed by a dinner engagement to leave before they did, I suggested that if either of them were in Milan they should come out to lunch with us at Gernetto. If after this brief meeting I was to see more of one than the other of the two, I would have supposed it more likely to have been Freya since we had found that we had friends in common. As it turned out it was only during a short period three years later that we were to get to know her at all well, whereas with Peggy, who took up my invitation soon afterwards, we kept up a friendship over many years during which we exchanged visits, the last when she stayed with us in England only a few months before her death.

She came to lunch at Gernetto with Marini Marino and his wife, Marina, with whom we had become close friends. Early in their married life they had taken an apartment overlooking a cavalry barracks. With the subject daily before him, obsessed by the relationship between horse and rider, Marino had begun the series of large sculptures in wood and bronze for which he was later to become famous.

At the time of the lunch party Peggy had just moved into the Palazzo Venier dei Leoni next to the Ca'Dario on the Grand Canal. It had a large garden at the back in which she was planning to have a sculpture exhibition. After lunch, on returning to Milan, she went with Marino to his studio where he agreed to lend her a bronze horse and rider for the exhibition. She liked it so much that she bought it and had it placed on the terrace in front of the *palazzo*. At his suggestion to which Peggy, always happy to shock, enthusiastically agreed, he added a rampant phallus to the horseman.

In a letter thanking us for the lunch party Peggy invited us to stay with her in Venice. Although we had both enjoyed her visit we felt that we were more likely to be at ease when entertaining her than as her guest. We wrote back declining the invitation with the valid excuse that we couldn't leave Charles and David, aged seven and five, on their own at Gernetto. She replied by return that we should bring the children with us. Hesitant about accepting for ourselves, we were even more doubtful about how a family visit might turn out, but not wishing to offend her we accepted and a weekend was agreed upon.

From the start all went better than we could have hoped. On arrival at the *palazzo*, as Peggy greeted us in the hall, the children came out with remarks which, had they been rehearsed beforehand, could not have been better calculated to please her. Charles, who must have heard us say that she had grandchildren, announced that Mrs Guggenheim did not look like a grandmother. This was most likely prompted not by her appearing too young, as she happily took it, but by her garish make-up. Next, David, precociously responsive to art, ignoring his hostess as he gazed at the paintings on the walls, exclaimed: 'What beautiful pictures!'

After that the weekend went splendidly but for an awkward moment when one of Peggy's Tibetan terriers had a surreptitious nip at Charles's leg.

To be living so intimately with the collection, at that time hung all over the *palazzo*, was as exciting as it was relaxing to sit in the tree-shaded garden or in the sun on the roof terrace overlooking the Grand Canal. In the afternoons Peggy, a most thoughtful hostess, took the children off in her gondola leaving us free to ramble about the city as we chose. When we left she insisted that we should stay with her whenever we came to Venice, an invitation so warmly offered that we were encouraged to accept it, though without the children, on several occasions.

The pleasures of being her guest were many, not least to be given a bedroom with paintings by such artists as Miró and Tanguy on the walls, to wake in the mornings to see the water of the canal reflected like animated marble on the ceiling and to eat breakfast sitting on the broad window ledge while watching the gondolas and other craft passing by only a few feet below eye level. Then at meals in the dining-room, according to which side of the table one was placed, one could contemplate at the risk of conversational lapses a superb cubist Braque or Picasso's great painting of *Bathers on a Beach*.

The collection was not as yet open to the public, but small groups with acceptable credentials were allowed to view it by appointment. Sometimes when talking over coffee after lunch in the salon one had the sensation of taking part in a play as visitors, intent on listening as well as looking, lingered to admire a Léger conveniently placed for keeping an ear cocked to the conversation. As they were allowed into every room, taking an afternoon siesta risked waking up to find the bed surrounded by the backs of a visiting group who, while pretending not to have noticed one's presence, tiptoed with hushed comments from picture to picture.

Fellow guests whether staying or invited for meals, strange, raffish, glamourous, famous – some with all these attributes – were often but not always a bonus. And then, of course, there was Peggy herself.

If not strange, she was certainly unusual. We had a number of American friends, but none were in the least like her. A New Yorker from a rich Jewish enclave against which she had rebelled, but not to the extent of forgoing her inheritance, her preference, although some of those closest to her were American, was for Europe and Europeans. This did not prevent her from being unmistakeably American both in manner and speech if far from so in the views she was liable to come out with. That she was a touch raffish was undeniable (this was how she was seen at the time by scandalised Venetian society) though much less so, as her memoirs were to reveal to us, than she had been in her wilder past. Glamourous at fifty she was not, though from Man Ray's photographs she must have been when younger, especially before plastic surgery on her nose went disastrously wrong. Sexy and intent upon appearing so still she had kept her figure but did not improve her looks by her mop-like hairstyle and excessive use of lipstick. Without question famous for her collection alone and confident of the importance of what she had achieved, she was impervious to gossip which claimed that she was less interested in art than in collecting the artists as lovers.

If the *palazzo,* brimming with light reflected from the Grand

Canal, had, apart from the pictures on its walls, a dynamic quality of its own, it was matched by the life carried on inside it with its continuous flow of guests and visitors, among them celebrities of all kinds especially artists and writers. Not that Peggy was a dedicated lioniser, even less a snob, or like many of the super-rich only fully at ease in the company of others within their own financial bracket. Her likes and dislikes tended to be intuitive and spontaneous, uninfluenced by background, reputation or notoriety. Intent upon getting all she could out of the animated existence the palazzo encouraged, she loved to indulge her curiosity about people, especially those she had recently met for the first time, her scandalous speculations about their intimate lives no less diverting than her frank revelations about her own.

Generally in conversation she was erratic, making daring leaps from one subject to another, while her responses to views expressed were unpredictable, dictated, perhaps, by irrational prejudice or the recall of some undisclosed incident in her past. Intelligent, widely read but haphazardly educated, she was an alert listener, her contribution to a discussion being often confined to perceptive questioning. Her enjoyment of the company she was with was sometimes marred by her readiness to suspect slights or to involve herself in wrangles over money. Seldom completely relaxed she was wary – vulnerable as she felt herself to be as the heiress of a great fortune and with a name which spelt millions – of the motives not only of strangers who besieged her with dubious projects, but even old friends whose loyalty she valued.

Although by the time we first knew her she was not as volatile as she had been in the past she could make prodigious scenes when provoked. A comparatively mild one was when she peremptorily turned a young Californian out of the house after he had been tactless enough to ask her who had ghosted her memoirs. On another occasion a friend with whom she had quarrelled, having inveigled her into inviting him to lunch, brought with him, hoping for a reconciliation, a present of a pretty tortoiseshell box. As she took it from him she remarked that if it was genuine it would be almost unbreakable. Putting her theory to the test she hurled it onto the marble floor where it predictably shattered.

Despite the triumph she had had with her collection at the 1948

Biennale and her luck in being able to buy the Venier dei Leoni, the only building on the Grand Canal so devoid of interior decoration as to be fitting for the display of her pictures as its garden was for her sculptures, there was a restlessness about her and at times, for all the enthusiasm with which she threw herself into her Venetian venture, a touch of melancholy as if she was forever straining after a fulfilment which eluded her, a gaiety which rarely quite came up to its promise.

In her childhood, as described in her autobiography, she had been haunted by guilt at the amount of money washing around her. Once she had inherited her fortune she had spent lavishly, even crazily, but she had assuaged her nagging puritan streak by redeeming her excesses, as she saw it, once she had started collecting. Given to covert generosity for which she naturally got no credit, she was also capable of petty tightness over money which hurt her reputation. Prompted by her experience when she had first come to Europe she was hyper-sensitive to any hint of being sponged on. Her wariness had seen off many sharks but had lost her some genuine friends unjustifiably accused.

That our own relations with her survived this acid test was doubtless due to our exchange of visits, for as often as we stayed with her in Venice, once we had moved to a flat in the city, she stayed with us in Milan. The flat had only three bedrooms, our own, the children's and our maid's, but it had a large drawing-room with a comfortable sofa on which Peggy, in preference to staying in a hotel by herself, was perfectly content to be put up.

The first time she came was for a dress show at one of Milan's leading couturiers. Although she was interested in clothes and dressed effectively in a style of her own she could be disastrously misguided. This was particularly true in winter when she habitually wore a long loose-fitting coat of some shaggy not easily identifiable fur which, as people unkindly remarked, closely resembled that of her Tibetan terriers. This, combined with the exotic dangling earrings she favoured, produced an effect which was striking but hardly elegant. Leonora, who went with her to the show, was uncomfortably conscious of the critical stir her appearance caused. The other women present, sticklers for the fashion convention of the moment and dressed up in their most modish outfits, blatantly stared at her and exchanged contemptuous and quite audible comments. Though Peggy must have been aware of this she showed not the faintest concern, only shocking them further by making deprecating remarks about every garment displayed on the catwalk.

On one visit she came when her daughter, Pegeen, and son-in-law, Jean Hélion, both had exhibitions of their paintings in Milan. After the opening Peggy gave a dinner party to which we were invited. It was the only time we met Pegeen. She did not look like her mother but had the same nervy restlessness. Her father, Lawrence Vail, Peggy's first husband, came from his home in France to see the exhibitions. One evening he joined us at supper after the opera. He was already very drunk and at once started a violent quarrel with Carla Mazzoli, a friend of Peggy's, who was in the party. When he had worked himself into what seemed a simulated rather than genuine frenzy, he left the table to return with a pot of jam he had taken from the restaurant kitchen. Dipping his finger into the pot he tried, unsuccessfully, for we all intervened, to rub the jam into Carla's hair.

Another time Peggy came with her son, Sinbad, who lived in Paris where he was owner and editor of *Points,* a magazine which published short stories and poems by young, avant-garde writers some of whom later became famous. Educated in England at Bedales, he became a cricket fanatic and was proud of holding the rather recondite post of secretary to the Paris Cricket Club. Extremely likeable with a dry sense of humour, he had an openly declared hostility to art having suffered from a surfeit of it throughout his childhood. He was further prejudiced against it because he felt that his mother was not generous enough in supporting him and that if she could only be persuaded to sell one of her more valuable paintings and give him the proceeds, all his financial worries would be over.

Once after a visit she left me with what proved to be an embarrassing commission. As her passport had run out she asked me to take it to the American Consulate to be renewed. She admitted that she had tampered with it by changing the date of her birth as she did not want to risk her lover seeing the passport and finding out her real age. Unfortunately the official I saw was uncompromising. In vain I appealed to his sense of gallantry. Po-faced and adamant he refused to overlook the crudely inked-in change of date and even threatened to prosecute her for defacing an official document. I had to send it back to her assuring her that I'd tried all the diplomatic wiles I possessed to no effect and that to get the passport renewed she would have to apply for it in person.

Her lover at the time was a young Italian called Raoul Gregorovich. He came of a respectable family; his father was a judge, presumably with Yugoslav antecedents. After completing his military service he had been arrested for taking part in an armed robbery and had served a prison sentence in Venice. On release he had worked for a furrier in Milan. I do not know how Peggy first met him or how soon afterwards he was installed more or less permanently in the *palazzo*. He was extremely good-looking, had charm and was unfailingly polite. He appeared to be fond of Peggy and to be content to hover in a limbo, certainly remote from the servants – whereas they referred to her as 'la Signora', he did so as 'la Signora Peggy' – but not quite on the same level as her guests. This was mainly because he had no interest in art or any other topic likely to be discussed so that it was not easy for him to enter or be drawn into the conversation.

What he was really keen on was fast cars and flashy blondes. Of the first Peggy was aware and had bought a dashing sports car to please him; the second, whether or not she had any idea of it, he obviously did his best to keep from her. He was not always so discreet when away from Venice. On one occasion in Milan I only just managed to avoid meeting him face to face with the flashiest of blondes in the Galleria. Whatever the cause, by the time we left Milan, his relations with Peggy had become strained, but it was his love of fast cars which tragically ended it. Shortly after she had stayed with us in Cyprus, deeply stricken, she wrote to tell us that he had been killed in a motor accident.

We moved to Cyprus in the autumn of 1952. The house in the capital, Nicosia, which we inherited from my predecessor was modern, spacious and well-equipped, but in atmosphere depressingly soulless. From our bedroom window we looked down on to the back of a colonial bungalow of the type favoured by the British in India. It had the traditional tiled roof which overlapped all round to cover a wide verandah, but what most attracted us to it was its large, wild garden planted with orange, *nespole* and pomegranate trees. As it appeared to be unoccupied we wondered if it might be for rent. Walking round from our austerely named Gladstone Road to the more romantic sounding Byron Avenue on to which it faced, we ventured up the garden path on to the verandah. Peering in through the tall windows we could see that the rooms were well proportioned, had open fireplaces and high ceilings. The bathroom looked primitive as did the kitchen which, with the servants' quarters, was a few steps down from the verandah at the back.

Undaunted by these obvious shortcomings we called on the owner and asked if we could rent it, He agreed, though clearly astonished that we should want to live in what he regarded as a scarcely habitable antiquated shack. We had only just moved into it when Peggy wrote from Venice inviting herself to stay. We felt certain that she would appreciate the charm of the bungalow with its airy rooms and its garden which, if lacking in sculpture, was more exotic than her own. What worried us was how she would take to sharing with the family – by now we had a third son, Luke, only a year old – the starkly equipped bathroom with its ancient, claw-footed tub and water-heating apparatus which gave out a menacing roar when in action. The bathrooms in the Venier dei Leoni were rather special. Installed by Lady Castleross, a former owner, they had walls, floors and sunken baths of black marble embellished with gilded taps and fittings. We wouldn't have been offended if after one look at our own she had turned down our hospitality in favour of a nearby hotel, but to our relief it did not seem to bother her at all.

She travelled from Venice on an Italian ship which docked at Limassol in the south of the island. I drove to meet her on the normal road from Nicosia which I already knew. As it was rather tedious and unattractive, I decided to give Peggy the chance of experiencing some of the island's finest scenery by returning on the more round-about route over the Troodos mountains. I had not yet tried it myself, and was innocently unaware of how circuitous it would prove.

I picked up Peggy from off the boat, told her of my plan and left the town on the Troodos road. It soon started to rise steeply but, though no wider than the one I had come by, it was more skilfully engineered. All was going well and we were enjoying the ever-expanding view of the southern coastline when, just as the road began to level out before starting its downward swoop, we struck snow.

It was early in the year and the mountain's snow-capped peak was visible from Nicosia but I had not counted on it reaching so far down. As elsewhere on the island the narrow ribbon of tarmac was edged by deep ditches. Here they were filled with snow so that the tracks of other vehicles were the only guide to where the hard surface lay. Within sight a truck, which had skidded off the road, had been left rakishly abandoned with two wheels in the ditch. As much of the snow had been packed into ice, it seemed likely that we might similarly be stuck. When I suggested to Peggy that it would, perhaps, be safer to turn back, with the coolness she was to show years later at taking risks on more exotic journeys we were to make together, she insisted that we should drive on as she wanted to see the view from the other side of the mountain. The snow only lasted a mile to two but it slowed us down to a crawl. There was an alarming moment, apparently unnoticed by Peggy, when we were forced by a large lorry on to what must have been the very edge of the tarmac where instead of a ditch there was a sheer drop into the pine forest.

The views on the descent from the mountain did not disappoint but the road looped unmercifully from village to village so that it took us over four hours to reach Nicosia. If Peggy felt as exhausted as I did, she did not show it as she exclaimed enthusiastically to Leonora about the island's scenery.

It was not only the inadequacy of our bathroom which had made us anxious about her visit. Although we could show her some of the more accessible ancient sites such as Salamis and what remained of medieval Famagusta and the Crusader castles on the Kyrenia hills, we were doubtful about how otherwise we could keep her entertained. As compared to her life in Venice what was on offer in Cyprus was extremely dim. We need not have worried for she proved the easiest and most appreciative of guests. She was charmed by the bungalow and its garden, showed no qualms about the bathroom and appeared to enjoy family life with the children. She was enthusiastic about the sites we took her to see and, unlike Freya Stark a year later, did not try our patience by exhaustive photography or urge us to over-extended expeditions.

Evening entertainment was more difficult as there were few people, British or Cypriot, who shared her interests or presented rewarding subjects for diverting speculation. Realizing it a risk we took her to an ex-patriot party. Soon bored with the conversation and impatient that although there was music no one was dancing, she wickedly seized on the most stiff and self-conscious of colonial officials and forced him, tortured with embarrassment, to partner her in dance after dance for the rest of the evening.

An outing to Famagusta went better. We had invited Evangelos Louizes, a delightful and much travelled Greek Cypriot, to join us for dinner. As he often stopped in Venice and spent much of his time in Paris and London, they got on well. After dinner he took us to a cabaret. When the show was over he astonished the rather louche *habitués* of the place by whirling Peggy off on an expertly footed, old-fashioned waltz.

When I took her to meet Lawrence Durrell, who had only recently arrived on the island and was living in Kyrenia, she disconcerted me by hardly speaking at all, leaving the conversation almost entirely to Larry and myself. Afterwards when I remarked that I hoped she hadn't been bored, she replied that she couldn't have enjoyed herself more as there was nothing she liked better than listening to Englishmen talking. I have no recollection of what we talked about but, doubtless, it was Larry's contribution, lively and witty as he usually was, that had diverted her.

Whenever we had stayed with her in Venice we had always taken her a present and invited her to meals in restaurants. While staying with us in Milan she had reciprocated generously. Now she had brought with her a fine chalk and ink drawing by Tancredi, a young Italian protegé to whom she had lent part of her basement as a studio. While the drawing gave us and still gives us much pleasure, she sent us on her return to Venice with thanks for 'a heavenly week in Cyprus' another much appreciated gift: a copy of her early memoirs, *Out of This Century*.

The book was not easy to come by at the time as her family had been so horrified by what she had written about them that they had seized and destroyed every copy they could get hold of. When in 1960 she published her *Memoirs of an Art Addict*, she drew on the earlier book in an expurgated version. When her publishers suggested a reprint of it (it was not until after her death in 1980 that it was brought out in paperback), she refused on the grounds that it was 'too intimate'.

Intimate it certainly was by the standards of the day. Written in a style which was typically all her own and carried through with unflagging verve, it was considered by Herbert Read and Edwin Muir, the only literary personalities we then knew who had read it, a valuable contribution to the literature of the period.

Both her memoirs share the same title 'Gilt-edged childhood' for their opening chapters but her account in *Out of This Century* of her Guggenheim relations on her father's side and the Seligmans on her mother's went further in revealing the extent to which they had been knocked off balance – their behaviour at extremes included suicide and murder – by such a sudden and vast accumulation of riches. It was not surprising that her family had been outraged, but no less so that Peggy with the anarchic tendencies of her early years had rebelled against the bourgeois, if unconventional, Jewish milieu in which she had passed what she described as 'an extremely unhappy childhood'.

Once an independent heiress, though still chaperoned by her mother, she made a dash for Europe on an intensive and extended tour. Passionate about painting she read all Berenson's books and travelled to remote towns and villages where paintings he mentioned were to be found.

The tour ended in Paris where at the age of twenty-three she began to feel 'burdened' by her virginity. For the purpose of losing it and anxious to try out what she had seen depicted in the erotic frescoes at Pompeii, she settled on Lawrence Vail whom she had first met in New York when she had been attracted to him by his streaky blond hair, beak-like nose and wild behaviour. At his first move to seduce her, she had startled him by her readiness to acquiesce. Her virginity lost, she reflected that he must have had a tough time as she had demanded of him all she could recollect from Pompeii.

After a series of wild parties and hesitations on both sides, Vail proposed to her on the top of the Eiffel Tower and was accepted. There followed eight years of turbulent marriage during which, despite the birth of two children, the parties grew wilder, the tit-for-tat infidelities more numerous and the quarrels more violent, frequently ending by Vail rubbing marmalade into Peggy's hair as he had tried to rub jam into Carla Mazzoli's in Milan.

The marriage finally foundered when Peggy fell in love with John Holmes, an Englishman whom his friend, Edwin Muir, described as giving him 'a greater feeling of genius' than any other man he had known. Peggy counted this as the most serious and rewarding love affair of her life. It ended with Holmes's death while undergoing a minor operation.

Bored and lonely after the break-up of yet another love affair she accepted a friend's suggestion that she should open an art gallery in London. Influenced by Marcel Duchamp and guided by Herbert Read, with her 'Guggenheim Jeune' venture she developed her appreciation of contemporary art. While in *Out of This Century* she went into greater detail about her love affair with Samuel Beckett and Yves Tanguy and her liaison with and subsequent marriage to Max Ernst, her account of how she became a serious collector and escaped out of Vichy France to America with her collection differs little from that in her later *Memoirs of an Art Addict*.

Although the book did not come as a startling revelation to us since we had already heard stories of the way she had lived in her earlier years, we were amazed into admiration at the frankness and immediacy of the style in which she recorded her pre-war erotic racketing from lover to lover and from country to country throughout Europe.

Returning to England from Cyprus we took the same Italian ship as she had done and stayed with her a few days in Venice. While on a visit to London she came to lunch with us in the country on her way to friends in Gloucestershire, a journey we were to make with her in reverse, deeply anxious about her health, many years later.

When we moved to Mexico in 1958 we invited her to stay once we had settled in. That winter she suggested she might come before going to New York. At the time Leonora was in England with the children while I was about to leave for Guatemala and Peru. To my letter explaining the situation she replied that she would like to travel with me, but she confused the dates and arrived at one o'clock in the morning on the day I was to leave. Her taxi driver woke me and probably the whole neighbourhood by banging with a monkey wrench on the metal panels of our garden door making a noise like stage thunder. Luckily I managed to get a seat for her on the plane on which I was already booked.

Although we had found her such an easy guest in Cyprus, I had misgivings about how she might turn out as a travelling companion. These proved to be groundless for she fitted in with my plans and when diverging from them did so without fuss or causing inconvenience. Uncomplaining, she put up with primitive hotels when necessary and was unperturbed by risky flights in ropey aircraft. We agreed from the start to share our expenses equably and never came near to falling out over who paid for what. But I was careful to keep accounts, knowing the complex she had about being done down even over the most trivial amounts.

How obsessively this could take hold of her was demonstrated by an incident in the hotel in Guatemala City. At the weekend we decided to go up to Chichicastenango, a hill village famous for its Sunday market. It was already a tourist attraction but there were few tourists about so that we were able to book rooms in a hotel recommended for its comfort and good food. The village was about a hundred miles from the city, the road to it winding up through the hills to a height of six thousand feet. We hired a taxi for the early afternoon. It was already waiting when Peggy came down to the hotel lobby with some letters to post. The transaction with the girl, little more than a child, at the counter was complicated as some of the letters were for Mexico, others for the United States and Europe. The girl became confused and Peggy started arguing with her until I intervened pointing out that unless we left at once it would be dark before we reached the village.

From the moment we set off Peggy was unusually silent and appeared deeply preoccupied. I had no idea what was troubling her and only hoped that it was nothing I had said or done. When we stopped for coffee beside Lake Atitlán she hardly seemed to take in the beauty of its still blue surface mirroring the numerous volcanoes which surrounded it.

As a result of our late start the sun had already begun to set when we left the lake shore and began the ascent into the highlands. At the first steep incline the taxi juddered and we only just reached the top. As we continued to climb its engine repeated this unpromising performance. We were by now in fairly wild country, the road enclosed by jungly vegetation except where the land fell sheer away giving glimpses of valleys so deep that they were already benighted. Half way up a particularly steep gradient the taxi juddered, stopped and even rolled back a few yards. At this moment of crisis Peggy, who had appeared oblivious to our halting progress, suddenly grabbed my arm and announced that after checking it through three times in her head she was convinced that the stamp girl had done her out of five cents.

I was too concerned with our predicament to be sympathetic. I had noticed that the driver had not once changed gear and had assumed that there must be something wrong with the gear box. Questioned as to what the trouble was he shrugged his shoulders declaring that he had never known the engine to behave in such a way before. He then admitted that it was the first time he had driven other than on the level streets of the city. With no experience of hill-climbing it hadn't occurred to him to change gear when the engine had faltered. I tried to persuade him to let me drive but fear of losing face kept him clutching the wheel. As a compromise he let me sit beside him to prompt him whenever a change of gear was needed.

It was dark by the time we reached the village and stopped at the hotel. This proved to be all that we had been led to expect of it. Furnished in the colonial style it had pleasant snug rooms with log fires. The food was good by Guatemalan standards but the dinner was spoilt for me by Peggy insisting on going over the whole stamp transaction while we were eating. The next morning the brilliant colours and exotic wares of the Indian market put it out of her mind, but in the afternoon on the way back, the nearer we got to the city, the more pensive she became. On arriving at the hotel she pounced on the stamp girl who, too terrified to argue, ducked behind the counter as she handed over the five cents.

The next day we went to Tikal, the site of an ancient Mayan city deep in the Peten rain forest. As yet there were no tourist flights so we booked on an old Dakota which tree-hopped from one forest settlement to another. That at Tikal must have been one of the smallest consisting only of a few bamboo huts, but the archaeological site was nearby. The plane bumped down on a rough grass patch sending chickens rocketing from under its wings.

The head attendant at the ruins, who had come down to collect a package off the plane, guided us to the camp, allotted us rooms in the rest house and, at Peggy's invitation, joined us for a drink in the canteen. He was tall for an Indian and handsome with the typical downward-curving nose of the Maya people. Afterwards he showed us round the site with its great pyramids rising out of the forest to be topped by stone sanctuaries islanded in a sea of foliage.

It struck me as I clambered up a pyramid or two that Peggy, who remained below, was as interested in our guide as she was in the ruins. That evening she confessed to me how attractive she had found him, possessing, as he did, what was for her the essential sexually arousing feature in male physiognomy: a beak-like nose. Of her lovers the only two we had met, Lawrence Vail and Raoul Gregorovitch both had such noses. In her memoirs she described John Holmes's nose as straight. Max Ernst preferred to have his picture taken full face, but from two of Lee Miller's photographs of him, in which his face is turned slightly to one side his nose appears as sharply curved as an eagles claw.

The ancient Maya were very proud of their noses even adding to their prominence by artificial means. Sitting over coffee in the steamy depth of the rain forest I was tempted to imagine how Peggy, had she been born back in classical Tikal, reacting to a surfeit of beak-like noses, might have decamped, perverse and headstrong as in her *Out of This Century* days, to join the not-so-far-away Olmecs whose noses, as featured in immense stone-sculptured heads, were, for an Amerindian people, remarkably flat.

If I had been disconcerted by her concern at being cheated out of five cents by the stamp girl in Guatemala, I was even more so by her failure to make any concessions in the clothes she wore to the conditions we might expect to meet with on our travels. However hot and humid the climate or tropically exuberant the vegetation with its attendant threat of snake or insect bites, she dressed, though in materials that may have been lighter, much as for any normally social day in her *palazzo* complete with fantastic earrings and ample jewellery – some but not all of it fake – down to her beautiful, slipper-like shoes which not only failed to support her rickety ankles but offered no protection from blood-suckers or poisoned fangs.

In Chichicastenango where the Indians wore gaily coloured clothes and were already prospering from tourists, she had mingled in the crowd without being disquieteningly conspicuous, but in the market at Cusco in Peru the effect was more disturbing. Whereas in Guatemala the Indians had adopted at the time of the conquest the costumes of the Spanish based on the jackets of the military or the breeches, waistcoats and head-kerchiefs of the sailors, in Peru the *conquistadores* had forced the Inca people into the contemporary garb of Spanish domestics, a dour outfit well matched to the abject mien of the modern peasantry condemned to lives of poverty and brutish exploitation. As we moved among the dismal assembly of women huddled on the ground, their wares laid out before them, Peggy was genuinely shocked, exclaiming that she was amazed that the authorities encouraged foreigners to visit the market when it was the scene of such wretchedness. But it did not occur to her on this as on similar occasions that, apart from how she was dressed, the wearing of so much jewellery might be seen by the Indians as a callous affront or a calculated provocation. Leonora, accompanying her later to the market in Oaxaca when, in addition to the jewellery she usually wore, she had put on gold ankle-bracelets, and remarking how heedless she was of the hostile glances directed towards her, was reminded of her indifference to the scoffing of the fashionable females, years before, at the Milanese dress show.

It was not that she was insensitive, as many rich and not-so-rich tourists are, to the element of poverty contributing to the picturesque, but it was in the essence of her character that she was incapable of the duplicity of presenting herself other than in the mode which came naturally to her and which she had made her own. When visiting the Maya ruins at Palenque in southern Mexico it showed what it could let her in for when worn as jungle togs and how glaringly inappropriate it could appear in the primitive setting of a poor and remote Indian village.

At that time it was not possible to reach Palenque by road so we hired a light aircraft in Villahermosa. From the strip where it landed we had to climb up a steep slope to reach the ruins. They were surrounded by deep jungle on three sides, the fourth being open to the plain below which stretched away to Villahermosa and the sea. In her *Confessions of an Art Addict* she was to describe Palenque as the most impressive of the pre-Columbian sites she saw in Mexico. 'The setting was wild and beautiful and the sculpture and architecture thrilling.'

After the solitary Indian guard had shown us round we lingered on through the afternoon risking sorties into the thick grass on the fringe of the site to get views of the ruins from every possible angle. As evening came on we collected our bags from the guard's hut and took the track which led to the village. He had told us that there were two small hotels on the outskirts, one owned by a German, the other by a Mexican. We decided on the latter where we were given stark but adequate bedrooms with showers adjoining. We agreed to meet in an hour for dinner.

Down before Peggy I was dismayed to learn that breakfast was the only meal served in the hotel and that there was no restaurant in the village. When Peggy joined me and I explained our dilemma, although we had only had a snack before leaving Villahermosa, she gallantly denied that she was in the least hungry. Taking pity on us the proprietor suggested we might try the village shoe shop as the owner, if he had sufficient food in store, was sometimes willing to provide scratch meals for stranded travellers.

Armed with a small torch I had brought with me we set out to find the shoe shop. The path from the hotel to the village was easy-going, but what passed for a street between the houses was no more than a deeply rutted track abounding in loose stones. At the moment we reached it my torch gave out and the intense, almost tangible, dark of a moonless tropical night closed in on us. There was scarcely a light in a window to guide us. We might have taken the village for dead but for an occasional bare-foot Indian, ghost-like in customary white shirt and trousers, gliding silently past as we groped our way on. We had almost despaired of finding the shop when rounding a corner we saw an open doorway lit from inside by an acetylene lamp which threw a bright rectangle on to the street.

When we reached it, looking inside, we saw shelves stacked with shoe-boxes and in the middle of the room three small tables set with chairs. The shop was empty, but as we entered, the owner appeared from the back. To our request for a meal he replied that he had only eggs and beans to offer. While he retired to the kitchen to give our order to his wife, we sat down opposite each other at one of the tables. Peggy was backed by a wall of shoe-boxes a few feet behind her. She had changed for the evening into a kimono-style dress patterned in peacock greens and blues with which she was wearing the inevitable dangling earrings, array of jewellery and soft leather shoes.

As we sat waiting a whole family of Indians, father, mother and four children, stopped outside and, made shy by our presence, hesitated on the doorstep. When the shopkeeper returned he encouraged them to come in. Very poorly clothed and all barefoot, they quietly settled in a huddle on the floor in front of the wall of shoe-boxes behind Peggy's chair. After assuring us that our meal would soon be ready and explaining that the peasant family had come in to buy the mother her first pair of shoes, the shopkeeper picked out an assortment of boxes from the shelves. With the patience demanded by the importance of the occasion he set about the trial-and-error process of fitting shoes to feet with toes flattened and soles calloused from being walked on for half a lifetime unshod.

Seated with her back towards it Peggy saw nothing of this touching scene. The Indians, for their part, if they glimpsed them under the table, doubtless dismissed her own shoes – made for her at heaven knows what cost! – as crazily impractical. This they again proved to be when, our meal over, we set off back up the village street with Peggy clutching my arm, her ankles unsupported, as she tottered over the treacherous surface.

In the morning at breakfast we were again faced with eggs and beans. Peggy was as uncomplaining as ever, but did casually remark that she had picked up crab lice in the lavatory adjoining her bedroom. I was a little surprised that she should have known what crab lice – not infrequently met with in my army days – looked like, but she explained that there had been a plague of them in the bathing huts on the Lido. She stretched out her leg to show the marks they had left round her ankle. Spotting one still clinging above her heel I identified it, before brushing it off, as the larger kind of jungle tic. I suggested that she might have picked them up in the long grass beside the ruins. Why hadn't I got any? she asked. I pointed to the boots I was wearing. Those elegant shoes had let her down again.

By the time we got back from Peru, Leonora had returned from England. She had already seen Leonora Carrington, the English surrealist painter with whom we had become close friends.

Though little known in England, she had been accepted in Paris with her highly individual talent, fantastic imagination and striking beauty as one of the most uniquely gifted and arresting personalities within the surrealist group. She had moved to Mexico in the forties and had come to be regarded by the Mexicans as one of their leading artists.

When Leonora told her that Peggy was coming to stay with us, her response had been more enthusiastic than might have been expected. Putting on her jolly-hockey-girl's voice, acquired at the exclusive convent school from which she had been expelled for subversive behaviour, she exclaimed: 'Good old Peggy! I'd love to see her again!'

This was generous considering their past relationship. Rebelling against her rich, Lancashire textile-manufacturing family background and Catholic upbringing Leonora Carrington had broken free to study painting in London. When Max Ernst had an exhibition at a London gallery in 1937, they met at a party, fell in love and eloped to Paris. At the outbreak of war they had moved south with other surrealists to St-Martin-d'Ardèche. Then Ernst was interned by the Vichy government. Leonora was shocked into a severe breakdown which led to her being incarcerated in a mental institution in Spain. She managed to escape to Lisbon where she met Ernst by chance in the street. He had been released from the internment camp and was living with Peggy who was arranging for their flight to America. There followed weeks of triangular agonizing until Peggy and Ernst obtained passages on a clipper to New York. Left in Lisbon, Leonora married a Mexican diplomat which gave her the right to a visa for the United States. Shortly after arriving in New York she again met Ernst by chance. By then he was married to Peggy. The tangle between the three of them was renewed and only ended when Leonora left for Mexico and Ernst was carried off by the American surrealist, Dorothea Tanning.

When we told Peggy that Leonora would like to see her again and suggested a visit to her studio, she agreed to go but less out of a wish to see her former rival than to have the opportunity of buying one of her pictures for the collection. The visit was a disaster. From the moment we entered the studio, Peggy lapsed into a sullen silence, leaving the two Leonoras and myself to keep an uneasy conversation going. We left after twenty minutes without Peggy having asked to see Leonora's paintings or hinting that she might like to buy one.

We had assumed that on seeing Leonora again she had been too painfully reminded of the part she had played in breaking up her marriage with Ernst, but at dinner that evening she revealed quite a different reason for her behaviour.

As a teenager Pegeen had gone with friends for a holiday in Acapulco. When the others left, Pegeen had stayed behind and, as reported to Leonora, was living on the beach with one of the boys who made high dives off the cliffs to earn pesos from the tourists. She had sent Peggy a telegram warning her of the danger she believed Pegeen to be in and the need for her to be rescued. The story, according to Peggy, had proved false. On seeing Leonora again she had been reminded of the anguish the telegram had caused her and had decided that a reconciliation was impossible.

Whatever Pegeen had been up to on her own in Acapulco, Leonora had been genuinely concerned about her, but Peggy had taken the telegram as a malicious attempt to show her up as an irresponsible mother. This must have been all the more troubling for her since it was a charge to which she must have known she had been vulnerable in her early, turbulent years.

Strong as her feelings clearly were about Leonora's behaviour, they did not make her change her mind about buying one of her pictures. Returning to England before moving to Brussels we took with us two of Leonora's paintings which Arthur Jefferies had agreed to exhibit in his London gallery. He was a friend of Peggy's and must have told her of the pictures he had for sale. She bought one of them apparently without being concerned at having to pay much more for it than if she had bought it direct from Leonora in her studio.

While we were living in Brussels Peggy stayed with us for a few days on her way from Venice to make a second visit to Mexico as the guest of Robert Brady in Cuernivaca. Two days after we had seen her off at the airport we read in the newspaper that Pegeen had died of an overdose of sleeping pills in her Paris flat. It appeared from the account that she had committed suicide.

Some years later when Robert Brady visited us in Bangkok he described the terrible hours he had spent with Peggy after the news of Pegeen's death had reached her on the evening of her arrival in Cuernivaca. Dry-eyed but utterly distraught she had stayed up all night agonizing over recent events in Pegeen's disturbed existence, desperate to convince herself that the overdose must have been an accident since she had been far too devoted to her children to have deliberately abandoned them by taking her own life.

Following the break up of her marriage with Hélion, who left her for Sinbad's first wife, Pegeen had several unsatisfactory love affairs including one with Tancredi, Peggy's young, mentally unbalanced protegé who, just as the success of his career as a painter was assured, committed suicide. Eventually she married an Englishman of whom Peggy so disapproved that, by some accounts, she had refused to help her though she had been living in Venice in considerable emotional and financial distress. After ten fraught years Pegeen wanted a divorce but this was opposed by her husband. For some months before her death they had been living apart, Pegeen in Paris where her children were at school, her husband in Venice. After an incident with the Italian police, he had gone to join her.

In adversity, as when she felt she had been cheated, it was in Peggy's nature to fight back. In New York her lawyer, Bernard Reiss, had pressed me to try to dissuade her from bringing a lawsuit against Lee Pollock, Jackson Pollock's widow, over some paintings in her possession which Peggy believed to be rightly hers under a contract she had had with the artist. Now in reply to our letter of condolence she wrote not only of how devastated she was by the tragedy and how she felt it would haunt her for the rest of her life, but of her determination to bring a case against Pegeen's husband for having made no attempt to save her. On his arrival in Paris, they had had a violent quarrel. Both had been drinking and it was alcohol combined with the pills which had proved fatal. If her husband had acted quickly, so she claimed, Pegeen's death could have been averted. Interrogated by the police he had told so many conflicting stories that he had laid himself open to the charge of wilful neglect to save life, a criminal offence under French law. Peggy's one consolation was that the family had managed to obtain custody of the children.

I do not know if the charge was proceeded with but the effect of Pegeen's death on her mother was profound and lasting. Certainly when we saw her next some five years later she was greatly changed.

After we moved from Brussels to Bangkok in 1967 she planned to come to stay with us following a tour in India but had to cancel her visit on hearing from Venice that her *palazzo* needed urgent structural repairs. It was only after we went to live in Paris in 1970 that we saw her again whenever she came to stay with Sinbad and his delightful English wife – another Peggy – in their house near the Bois de Boulogne.

Sinbad, the survivor of what must have been, at best, an unsettled childhood, had developed with his drily ironical view of life, a more stable personality than his sister's. He had abandoned his magazine *Points* many years before, rounding it off with a collection of its best short stories. Fanatical as ever about the game he had retained his secretaryship of the Paris Cricket Club. Hope lost of his mother ever selling one of her pictures to help him out financially, he had taken a job with an insurance company. He had always had a closer relationship with his father, Lawrence Vail, than with his mother, but was, perhaps, on better terms with her in those later years (she got on very well with his second wife) than at any time in the past.

Seeing Peggy again at the Vails or when she came to our apartment in the rue de Varenne we found that with age – she was now well into her seventies – if she had lost the rapacious zest for life of her earlier years, she was still as curious about people and as shrewdly questioning. She had stopped dying her hair and wore it in a style which, as it turned from grey to white, made her look far more distinguished. In manner, especially at any social gathering, she could be almost staid with a touch of the *grande dame* about her in her awareness of herself as a sought-after celebrity. The tendency she had always had to lapse into moments of brooding was now more in evidence. She only once talked to us about Pegeen and then with a reluctant reflection as to whether she ought to have treated her more sympathetically in her emotional entanglements. Perhaps to ease her conscience she had set herself a goal in the pursuit of which her life in Venice had taken, at least out of season, an almost Spartan turn, as we were to discover for ourselves when she invited us to stay with her one Easter.

In the years since we had last seen the *palazzo* there had been considerable changes. Permission had been given for the building of a pavilion in the garden in which the surrealist paintings and sculptures were handsomely displayed. This gave more space for the pictures hung in the *palazzo* itself. It also made it easier to allow access to the public who, unlike the select visitors in the past, were excluded from the bedrooms so that guests could enjoy a siesta without the risk of being disturbed. The only change which disappointed was the placing of iron grills over the windows, made necessary following the theft of several paintings, which were subsequently recovered. Though of a design in keeping with the period of the building they gave a caged-in effect to the interior and took away from the pleasure of breakfasting on the window ledge of one's bedroom while watching the traffic on the Grand Canal.

It was too early in the season for the collection to be open to the public so that we had the *palazzo* and all that it had to offer to ourselves and then, of course, there was Venice. Peggy encouraged us to go out as much as we liked but we spent the mornings enjoyably sitting with her in the sun on the roof terrace, keeping our expeditions to the afternoons. She only went with us when we took her to a restaurant for lunch or when we were invited for drinks with friends. The difficulty she already had in walking she put down to rheumatism. If she sensed that her condition was more serious, she never hinted at it although she often appeared to be in considerable pain.

While the spring sunshine was pleasantly warm to sit out in, the temperature fell sharply towards sunset. Only then in the evening of the first day of our visit did we realize that the central heating was turned off. It was chilly in the dining-room though reasonably warm in the salon when we sat round the fire after dinner, but once we were in our bedroom we were frozen. Even with coats and other clothes piled on top of us we were kept awake shivering most of the night. The next day we asked Peggy for an electric fire. She gave us a small one with three bars warning us that if we used more than one bar all the lights would be fused. When driven by the cold we risked it and turned on all three. The lights did not flicker.

It was not only on the central heating that Peggy was economizing. We ate well enough, but she went over in minute detail the food and other household bills presented to her each morning by the two rather disagreeable servants of whose wasteful and dishonest practices she frequently complained. She had always had the reputation of being close with her money, but as we had personally found her unfailingly, if not extravagantly, generous, this obsessive penny-pinching came as a shock. Once we had proved it safe to use all three bars of our fire, it would have taken nothing from our enjoyment of the visit, had it not worried us that when on her own she might make herself ill by even more extreme economies.

On the evening before we left we told her of our disquiet as tactfully as we could. She then revealed how she had vowed to herself to save enough money to ensure that her grandchildren – there were, I think, seven of them – would each inherit a million dollars when she died. At the time it was a significant sum and was not so easily raised given that the collection was sacrosanct. It evidently did not occur to her, even when recollecting her own unhappy gilded childhood and how, in spite of their wealth, the Gugenheims and Seligmans had not been without their troubles and tragedies, that these last remnants of the gilt which had been her share and which she was hoarding to the detriment of her physical comfort and, possibly, her health, might not necessarily turn out to be a guarantee of her grandchildren's ultimate happiness.

The following winter she came to Paris to spend Christmas with Sinbad. They had a family party on New Year's Eve to which they invited us. This gave us the opportunity of meeting some of the grandchildren and seeing Peggy in a role which it would have been difficult to imagine her taking on, after a reading of *Out of This Century* or with our own recollection of her life in Venice when we had first known her: that of the dignified, even awesome, Jewish matriarch at the head of her fond, but apprehensively reverential, family.

After supper she was seated in the chair of honour at one end of the drawing-room surrounded by the adults in the party some of whose relationship to her was for us, the only outsiders present, obscure, while the younger grandchildren put on at the other end of the room a charming entertainment organized by Sinbad's wife.

After we left Paris to live in England we kept in touch with Peggy, planning visits which for one reason or another failed to come off. In September 1976 when we had just returned from a long trip abroad she sent us an invitation which was more pressing than usual and proposed firm dates for us to stay with her the following month. We had already spent that year more than we normally allowed ourselves on foreign travel and after having been away for so long had found much to be done in the house and garden before winter. We wrote back explaining our situation and suggesting that we should put off our visit until the spring. To our astonishment we were rung up a few days later by a friend of Peggy's in Brighton to say that she had written to her asking her to buy tickets for us to fly out to Venice. Embarrassed by her offer since we could have perfectly well paid for the flight ourselves, we rang her up protesting at the generosity which she made light of. As she would clearly have been offended if we had turned it down we agreed to the dates for our visit which she had suggested.

It was mid-October when we arrived. The weather was still warm but unsettled with days of sunshine and others of rain and gloom. We found Peggy in rather low spirits and in poor health still complaining of rheumatism which made it impossible for her to walk more than a few yards without stopping to rest. Her obsession with saving for her grandchildren was now carried to even greater excess. The *palazzo* had begun to have a run-down look. She had only one servant, a rather slatternly cook-house-keeper with whom she bickered over the bills. Her private gondola of which she had written to us a year before that it was her greatest consolation in her old age had been, at least for the time being, dispensed with. Anxious to make the afternoon opening of the collection a paying concern, she would sit at a table in the hall, placed clear of the Calder mobile, intent on selling as many catalogues as she could to the visitors who came crowding in.

She had a young American staying at the house who was acting as her secretary. This gave her some company other than that of her servant, but his role was vague and he had a social life of his own which often took him out during the day and almost every evening. When the collection closed to the public at the end of the month, he would be leaving to spend the winter in New York.

Peggy had friends in Venice but few who lived there all the year round. Inevitably at her age many of those who had been closest to her both in America and Europe had died. We had come into

79

her life relatively late, but it was now almost thirty years since I had first met her with Freya Stark in the Ca'Dario, so that we were able to talk with her of the early days when she had first moved into the *palazzo* and the friends we had in common in both Venice and Milan. While we enjoyed our fortnight with her we were saddened by her evident loneliness, her obsessive economising and her increasing disability. When we left we hoped that our company had cheered her and that she felt sufficiently rewarded for her generosity in paying for us to fly out.

Soon afterwards she wrote to tell us that her illness had been diagnosed as arterial sclerosis. In the year which followed we had letters from her from various clinics where she was undergoing painful, but largely ineffectual 'cures'.

In August 1978 she celebrated her eightieth birthday and was, as she described in reply to our letter of congratulation, 'tremendously feted. The Grilli gave me a dinner for twenty persons at which Sinbad, the British Consul, the director of the Modern Museum and Joe Losey all gave speeches . . . I received many presents and fifty telegrams. The Pope was elected just as we crossed the Grand Canal and all the bells were ringing like mad. Unfortunately His Holiness and the Holy Shroud nearly pushed me off the television appearance which ended our evening at the Grilli . . . My sitting room looked like a funeral parlour so many flowers were there.'

With the letter she sent cuttings from the local newspapers. She was obviously deeply gratified by the warmth of the affection shown her by the people of Venice. When she had first moved into the *palazzo* they had been maliciously critical of her appearance and lifestyle. Only a few artists and still rarer critics with an understanding of modern art had appreciated the importance of her collection. As she records in her memoirs, Princess Pignatelli, representing the then prevailing view in Italian society, told her that if only she would throw her awful pictures into the Grand Canal she would have the most beautiful house in Venice.

All that was in the past. Thirty years on she was acknowledged as the city's most distinguished foreign resident and her collection, drawing crowds during the season, had become among so much else Venice had to offer, especially for the young, one of its outstanding attractions.

In the year following her birthday celebrations she came to London for a double cataract operation. I went to see her and found her with her sight not yet recovered although the operation had been successful. She was sitting in a chair in a poky little room in what seemed a rather second-rate nursing home possibly chosen by her as relatively inexpensive. While I was there, a nurse came in with her lunch, dumped the tray on the table in front of her and went out leaving her to feed herself although she was still too blind to make out what she was eating and could not have managed without my help. I advised her to complain to the surgeon when he came to see her. This she did and he arranged for her to be moved to a convalescent home on the outskirts of London where she was more comfortable and better looked after.

When she was sufficiently recovered she went to her friends in Gloucestershire, but rang up after a few days to ask if she could come to stay with us until she felt well enough to fly to Paris.

Although it was already March the weather was unseasonably cold. When we picked her up at her friend's house it was already beginning to snow. It went on snowing all the way on our drive back. By the next morning it was so deep that the hamlet in which we live was in danger of being cut off. With Peggy's health in such a precarious state, this was an added worry. In spite of all the painful treatment she had gone through she walked no better than when we had been with her in Venice. Now she told us what we had not known before, that she had recently been in hospital after a heart attack. As always she was an easy guest and remarkably cheerful but she tired quickly and spent much of the time in bed. When the snow melted we took her for drives in the countryside which she enjoyed although she was still having difficulty with her sight and found the glasses she had been given in London did little to help.

One evening we asked John Rothenstein, a former Director of the Tate Gallery who lived in a nearby village, to come for a drink. They had met at the 1948 Biennale and had got on so well that Peggy had considered leaving the collection to the Tate but had given up the idea when warned of the problems she would have with the Italian authorities. The evening was not a success. Perhaps because he had been too long retired from the art world, Rothenstein had little to contribute. Peggy, who had been looking forward to seeing him again, found him so boring that she soon dropped out of the conversation.

Since her arrival I had exchanged telephone calls with Sinbad. I had hoped that he would be able to come over to take her back to Paris, but as he was recovering from a serious illness, I agreed to travel with her myself. After ten days, when our local doctor considered her well enough to make the journey, I rang British Airways to book our seats. When I asked for a wheelchair to be ready for her at Heathrow, the official asked what was wrong with her. Imagining that he needed assurance that she was ill enough to qualify for a chair, I told him that she had arterial sclerosis. To my dismay he said that she would be considered too great a risk by the airline as she might have a heart attack on the flight. To have travelled by train and ferry would have put far too great a strain on her so I cancelled and made a fresh booking the next day without mentioning her need for a chair. Luckily, on arriving at Heathrow I managed to get her one without difficulty. Knowing that she was liable to have a heart attack I found the flight worrying, but we arrived without incident and were met by Sinbad's wife at the airport. The Vails pressed me to stay with them but with Sinbad ill I had thought it would put them to too much trouble and had arranged to spend the night with other friends.

I was relieved at having brought Peggy safely to Paris and her family, but saddened when it came to saying goodbye to her as, aware of how ill she was, I did not think it likely that I should see her again. She wrote to us while still in Paris to thank us for looking after her and later from Venice to tell us that she had got back safely, her eyesight much improved by glasses she had had prescribed in Paris. She did not write again but we kept in touch by telephone. Some months later she broke her ankle (those shoes again?) and was taken to a hospital near Padua for an operation. In December a mutual friend rang up from Venice to tell us that after another heart attack she had died.

Sinbad, grateful to us for having had her to stay after her operation and for getting her safely back to Paris, generously sent us some finely bound Dickens first editions from her library. She must have bought them during her first marriage for it was as Peggy Vail that she had written her name in the flyleaf of each volume. It was a name which in itself did not invoke anything of the Peggy we had known. With its innocent look on the page it could have been the choice of a romantic novelist for a chaste and virginal heroine. Certainly Peggy was neither virginal nor chaste at that time, nor was she innocent in the generally accepted sense of the word, yet there was, surely, more that a touch of it in the frankness with which she wrote about herself, successes and failures alike, without an apparent thought of how such uninhibited revelations might, by the malicious or genuinely outraged, be held against her.

But throughout her life, when evasiveness might have been to her advantage, her response, whether shrewd, impulsive or ingenuous, to no matter what situation or whatever turn a conversation might have taken, had always been characteristically careless of how it might reflect on herself.

Her obduracy in contention and her warmth in friendship, her generosity and her stinginess, her plunges into gloom and wholehearted abandonment to laughter, her puritan streak and her reckless addiction to the erotic were all contradictions of the essence of her personalty. The collection, too, was a personal one, for though she had been advised by Duchamp, Read and others, it owed much more than her detractors were prepared to admit to her own flare and enthusiasm.

With her luck in being able to buy the Venier dei Leoni, her aptitude for enjoying to the full what her life in Venice had to offer and with the money to travel where she pleased and to indulge herself as she chose, there was, for all her apparent hard-headed hedonism, an unexpectedly vulnerable side to her. We had seen how deeply Pegeen's death had effected her and had been disturbed by the extent of her subsequent scrimping in her daily life, as we had been touched by the naivety of her belief that by hoarding what remained of her share of the Guggenheim fortune she could ensure the future happiness of those to whom she planned to leave it.

With all the vagaries of her character, Peggy had a vitality and a readiness to take anything on which made her generally good fun to be with. Even on our later visits, if the *palazzo* had lost much of its earlier glamour, there could have been no better way of enjoying Venice than as her guest. In turn when she had stayed with us in the different countries we had lived in she had, as a guest herself, been generous and undemanding, fitting in with our family life and appreciative of what we had been able to do to entertain her. We felt ourselves lucky to have had such a lasting friendship with her and to be left with so many varied and enjoyable, except for the sadness at the very end, recollections of the visits exchanged between us.

[6]

Dame Freya Stark
and How to Get Where You Want
to Go with a Little Help from
Your Friends

Following our move to Cyprus in 1952 it was not Peggy but Freya who was our first visitor from Italy. I had invited her that evening at the Ca'Dario to come to lunch at Gernetto but it was not until we had moved into a flat in Milan that she lunched with us while on a trip from her home in Asolo to make a round of the Milanese dress shops.

She told us that had she not chosen to be a writer and traveller she would like to have been a dress-designer. She certainly took a great interest in her clothes and bought them from the most expensive fashion houses. This was not strikingly apparent since her bundly shape ensured that whatever she wore, however elegant, had a decidedly homely look. That morning she had bought herself a hat. I had been told since first meeting her that she had been partially scalped as a young girl when her hair was caught in a loom at her parents' textile factory. The new hat served well in concealing the disfigurement. Shaped like an old-fashioned bee-hive it rose in a high dome above her head while its brim fitted closely over her ears. The effect was strange, for it seemed too ponderous for her dumpy figure, threatening at an injudicious nod to slip down and extinguish her like a candle-snuffer.

When I was next in Venice I had to go to a meeting in Udine. As Asolo was on the way I invited myself to lunch with Freya. A friend of Peggy's, Roloff Benny, a young Canadian painter, later to become a successful photographer, was staying at the *palazzo*.

As yet unpractised with a camera, he was intent on making a collection of drawings of famous people. He had never heard of Freya before but, once assured of her fame, he insisted on my ringing her up to ask her if I might bring him with me.

A few weeks before Freya had married Stewart Perowne, an historian and former diplomat she had known for many years and with whom she had many friends and interests in common. Freya must have been close on sixty and Perowne somewhat older. Doubtless because he had always enjoyed her company and appreciated better her intelligence and gifts as a writer, but with an eye, too, now that they were both no longer young, to an agreeable retirement at Asolo, he had sent her a telegram proposing that they should marry and live together as 'good friends'. Disregarding his accent on 'good friends' and innocently blind to his not so covert emotional inclinations, she had accepted the proposal by return with romantic enthusiasm. No sooner had she sent the telegram than she had summoned the village carpenter to make a matrimonial bed of ample proportions.

Asolo is an attractive village perched on a spur of the foothills rising to the west of the Veneto. The Villa Freya was situated at the end of the village with a garden which had a superb view over the plain towards Venice and the sea. As it was early summer and the sun was not too hot we had lunch outside.

Perowne, whom I had not met before, seemed to have quite settled himself into the role of host in what had been for so long exclusively Freya's home ground. Charmingly affable he gaily gabbled gossip about mutual friends. The tempo of Freya's conversation was very different. While often witty it was tellingly measured and reflective. Outclassed in sheer volume of talk by her husband, she was obviously not happy to find herself less listened to than forced to listen.

After lunch, as I was about to suggest that we ought to leave if I was to arrive in Udine in time for my appointment, Benny asked Freya if he could make a drawing of her. Far from taking this as presumption on the part of a young, unknown artist whom she had only just met for the first time, Freya was clearly flattered. Bridling, she asked him where he would like her to sit. He took a chair from round the table and placed it in full sunlight, but when she sat down he complained that her straw hat too deeply shadowed her face, adding that I had told him that she had a hat shaped like a beehive which might be more suitable. Suspecting that I had joked with him about the hat, which, indeed, I had, Freya gave me a cool look. I hurriedly assured her that I had only tried to describe its shape when recalling how well it had suited her. Mollified she went into the house and came back wearing it. The artist approved and, disregarding my impatience to be off, took almost an hour over the drawing before he was satisfied. It proved to be quite a good likeness. Freya was delighted and expecting, after the tedium of sitting for him, that he would give it her, was evidently put out when he only allowed her a moment to admire it before taking it back and putting it in his satchel.

On the road to Udine, speeding to get there on time, I felt that the visit had not been a success. Freya had been huffed by Benny's refusal to let her have the drawing and irritated at being out-talked by Perowne over lunch. We did not see her again while we were in Italy but had news of her from Osbert Lancaster whom, as a close friend, she had persuaded to decorate her bathroom in preparation for her marriage. He told us of her disappointment at Perowne's disinclination to join her in the bridal bed and that they were planning – but surely we must have misunderstood him! – a cycling holiday in the Caribbean. Soon afterwards we heard that they had separated, Freya complaining that being married to Perowne was like living with a permanent cocktail party.

We had only recently moved to Cyprus when she made the first and shortest of her two visits while we were on the island. One of the other guests at a lunch party we gave for her was Alex Shaw, a documentary film director who was making a film to encourage literacy among the Palestinian refugees in the Gaza strip. Freya attacked him fiercely about his work. With her affection and admiration for the illiterate nomads among whom she had travelled before the war she was convinced that if the refugees were to be taught to read and write they would lose their Arab identity and become victims of hot-headed propaganda. Alex held that if they remained illiterate they would have no hope of improving the appalling conditions in which they lived and would continue to be callously exploited.

One only had to read Freya's books to learn what she had found in the Arab way of life so attractive that she had wanted the clock to be stopped for the Gaza refugees. It was more difficult to imagine what the Arabs, always so ready to receive her hospitality, might have seen in her. Only after lunch was I to discover on returning to my office, at the time on the ground floor of a modern villa in which we were living, what an appeal a plain, dumpy English woman, bulging, from a western point of view, in all the wrong places, might have for the oriental eye.

My Armenian secretary was always extremely curious about our guests, leaving his desk to open the door a crack to peer out as they passed. Usually he was too discreet to make any remarks about them, but on this occasion he sprang from his chair, eyes alight, as he asked me who the beautiful woman was who had been our guest at lunch. I supposed him to be referring to Alex's wife, a slim and very attractive blonde. 'No! That other lady,' he corrected me, 'the one with the hat and the twinkling black eyes and the . . . ' He did not finish the sentence but indicated with a series of rounded gestures that it was also her figure which he had found seductive.

Enlightened by this reaction to her, I was left wondering if in her early travels, possessor of curves as voluptuous to them as to my Armenian, she had ever succumbed to the advances of the blue-eyed, hawk-nosed nomads she had encountered in the desert. If she had, it was easy to understand how her marriage to Perowne, intelligent and charming as he was, might have proved a disappointment.

We first heard from Austin Harrison, the distinguished British architect with whom we had become friends soon after our arrival, that Freya was intending a second visit. For some years Austin had been employed by the Colonial Office on projects for colleges and universities in Africa. His work had been admired for his skill in introducing features of the indigenous architecture into buildings both practical and attractive in design. Recently he had built himself a house in Lapithos, a village near Kyrenia, into which he had incorporated wide pointed arches round a courtyard in the Cypriot manner.

It was this reputation for successfully combining the traditional with the functional which had earned him an important but impossibly exacting commission: the plan for Nuffield College in Oxford which Lord Nuffield had insisted must have the character-

Paddy and Joan Leigh-Fermor in the library at Kardamyle

Peggy Guggenheim with the author.

Graham and Hilda Sabastian
at Coggershall..

Dame Freya Stark.

Sir Eugen Millington-Drake

Nānamoli Thera (Osbert Moore) at work on his translation from Pali at Doanduwra

istics of Cotswold village architecture along with a tower and spire to vie with those of existing colleges.

Whenever we had been to see him before, his plans for the project had been spread out on a table in his large living-room. Now all were cleared away and a suitcase by the door suggested his imminent departure. Tall, handsome and romantically distinguished with his neat white beard, he normally had the air of having everything about him well under control. He was the last person we would have expected to find rattled, but that was how he decidedly seemed as he greeted us. After explaining that he had not had time to put us off he told us that he was about to leave for Limassol to catch the first boat to the Piraeus. His sudden flight had been prompted by a letter from Freya proposing to stay with him for a month while she studied Turkish before making an expedition to Anatolia. She was an old friend of his whom he much admired, but the prospect of being stuck with her for such a long period had so unnerved him, knowing from past experience how exigent a guest she could be when once installed, he had decided on a dash to Athens to escape the ordeal.

Thwarted in her first choice of where to settle she turned to an amenable woman friend with a cottage on the outskirts of Kyrenia. This did not prove altogether satisfactory as her friend had neither the means, nor, possibly, the inclination, to entertain her, as she would have expected of Austin, with intellectual parties and excursions round the island.

However intrepid and self-reliant she may have been in her early travels, by this time, accepted by the Foreign Office establishment as an expert on the Middle East and a personality to be treated with respect, even cosseted, she had come to rely on the hospitality of ambassadors and on transport provided by embassy and consular officials. In colonial Cyprus she had no such advantage since the governor, though admirable in his rather limited way, was not easily approachable, while his officials were too lethargic to bother about outsiders who were unlikely to serve their immediate interests.

When she came to lunch with us soon after her arrival I inadvisedly let on that my office hours, starting early, allowed me four hours off in the afternoons to go for picnics or swimming from the Kyrenia beaches. Regretting how little she had seen of the island

since her friend had no car, she begged to be taken on our next
outing. Innocent of what we might be letting ourselves in for we
agreed to call at her friend's house to take her for a picnic in the
hills. We enjoyed her company but when the picnic was over she
insisted that if we were to drive a few miles further on we would
be able to climb up to one of the crusader castles. Although it was
rather more than a few miles, her persuasiveness won us over.
There was little left of the castle but, a keen photographer, she
took snaps of the ruins from every possible angle. By the time we
got back to Nicosia, after dropping her off in Kyrenia, I was half
an hour late at my office.

Encouraged by our acquiescence over the castle she took to
cajoling us into much longer expeditions at weekends, luring us on
from frescoed church to ancient site and from Gothic ruin to
Islamic shrine, so that with her meticulous photography it was
usually after dark when we got home.

Meanwhile her Turkish lessons were progressing. At the end of
one trip she left Leonora with a book of Turkish proverbs with
English translations, asking her to buy her a second copy in
Nicosia. Looking through it Leonora saw that she had marked the
proverbs she wanted to learn by heart. The one which she had
heavily underlined, 'the hen which lays a goose's egg bursts its
bottom', left us both trying to imagine the scene when she brought
it out to put down some too grasping or boastful Turk.

On leaving Cyprus she planned to stay with David Balfour, the
British consul in Izmir. He was an unusual character who had
collected religions rather like some men collect memberships of
different clubs. Converted from Anglican to Rome, he had been
sent on a mission to Moscow where he had promptly joined the
Orthodox church. Moving south he had spent some years as a
monk on Mount Athens before becoming chaplain to the King of
Greece. When the Germans invaded he had fled with the royal
entourage to Cairo. Once there he had doffed his Orthodoxy to
become a British diplomat. It was in this secular role that he had
returned to Athens after the war. The Athos monks had been
appalled by his conduct. When I toured the mountain myself, the
abbots of several monasteries asked me to tell him how shocked
they had been by his apostasy.

While Freya was still on the island, Graham Sebastian came to stay with us. He was also a friend of Balfour and was planning to stop with him in Izmir. In a letter agreeing to the date for his arrival Balfour wrote that he was threatened with a visit from Freya. The last time she had stayed with him, he complained, she had made him take her up and down the coast in his yacht looking at ancient sites. He was determined to resist being so exploited if she came again.

However frankly he may have tried to discourage her in correspondence, she stuck to her plan. Some weeks after she had left Cyprus she sent us a postcard thanking us for having helped her to see so much of the island. It ended with a flourish: 'I'm having a marvellous time on David's yacht!'

We saw her again two or three times at parties in London and once when Osbert Lancaster brought her to lunch with us in the country. Many years later we almost caught up with her in Afghanistan. One of the monuments we would like to have seen there was the minaret of Jam. Our French guide book was not encouraging: 'Si vous êtes plein d'ardeur et audace, si vous avez suivant le temps et si vous êtes en possession d'un véhicule rompu a toute épreuve . . .' Of the road to the minaret itself, it warned: 'La piste a été tracée de façon trés empirique par les paysans de la région et plus d'un automobiliste a rebroussé chemin avant d'atteindre le but.'

When I asked my colleague, Ken Pearson, if there was any chance that we might be able to get to see it, he told us that it was very inaccessible and the journey would take too long. Freya Stark, he added, who had just left Kabul after staying with him for a fortnight, had visited the minaret only a week or two before. 'How did she manage it?' we queried. 'Oh, the embassy sent her under escort with a couple of jeeps.'

That we were envious I have to admit. The travel book she brought out the following year was entitled *The Minaret of Jam*.

[7]

Sir Eugen Millington-Drake
and the Latin-American
Technique

In the spring of 1954, when we were living in Nicosia, I received a letter from Sir Eugen in which he wrote that his old friend, Lawrence Durrell, had suggested that he get in touch with me. He intended coming to Cyprus to see his daughter, Marie, who was having a house built for herself on the island. If I could arrange it, he would be very pleased to give a poetry recital during his visit.

I rang Larry, who was living in Kyrenia, to ask his advice. 'O yes,' he said, 'of course you must have him. He's a wonderful character. He was in charge of the British Council in Latin America. When he visited us in Argentina he used to make us do physical jerks on the roof before breakfast. He's just the man for you. You'll like him enormously.'

'What about the poetry reading?'

'Excellent! He's a marvellous actor. Puts everything into it. It'll go down splendidly with the boys from the English School.'

With some misgivings about the mixture of poetry and physical jerks I wrote back to Sir Eugen in Tripoli, where he was then living, accepting his offer and suggesting some dates. I had hardly sent the letter when a telegram arrived from a colleague in a neighbouring country warning me that Millington-Drake was on the move and strongly advising me against having anything to do with him. This was followed by telegrams from all over the Middle East carrying the same message and urging solidarity in a general boycott.

I rang Larry in alarm. I was not reassured by his chuckle. 'Oh, they're all so wet your people! You're the only one who'll appreciate him. He's a great hero really. He practically sank the *Graf Spee* single handed when he was Minister in Montevideo. He gives a wonderful lecture about it, too. He was a great athlete as a young man. Rowed for Eton and boxed as well. When he was Minister he arranged for a British champion to come out to fight with some local bruiser. The champion fell ill at the last moment so Millington-Drake went into the ring himself. He's a splendid man. Don't worry! I promise you won't regret inviting him.'

In the following months I exchanged frequent letters and cables with Sir Eugen. When the programme and dates were finally settled, I booked a room for him at the Dome Hotel in Kyrenia and wrote to assure him that it was one of the best on the island. He cabled back by return: 'Regret Dome not suitable. Please book single room without bath in small inexpensive pension.'

I was astonished by this request as I had been told by Larry that he was extremely rich. During the war when the Foreign Office had objected on grounds of economy to the length of his telegrams he had countered by sending even longer ones at his own expense. I rang Marie to ask her what I should do.

'Leave it to me,' she replied. 'He gets it into his head sometimes that he hasn't got any money. I'll say I booked a room at the Dome myself. He can blame me if he doesn't like it.'

On the day of his arrival I went to meet him at the airport. When he got off the plane, I had no difficulty in recognising him from Larry's description. Tall and extremely handsome with fine white hair, a pale complexion and regular features he advanced across the tarmac straight-backed as any guardsman but with the stride and poise of an athlete.

'Sir Eugen Millington-Drake?' I ventured when he was close enough; but he walked on unheeding, his blue eyes gazing into the sky. He might well have been deep in a run-through of his poetry recital. Trotting awkwardly alongside him I repeated my enquiry three times before I caught his attention. 'Ah, my dear fellow!' He swept round on me in a perfect demonstration of those courtly good manners popularly supposed to be the stock-in-trade of professional diplomats but quite beyond the range of the majority who seem to find it difficult to be even moderately polite. 'How delighted I am to meet you! How kind of you to come out all this way! I can't thank you enough for all the trouble you've taken and the splendid arrangements you've made.'

Lavish in his gratitude and compliments he continued in this vein with such charm and apparent sincerity that I found myself running round the customs shed like a frenzied boy scout in my eagerness to retrieve his luggage promptly. It was only when we got into the car and he heard me tell the chauffeur to drive to the Dome in Kyrenia that he broke off his praise for my deft handling of the customs and turned to me in alarm. 'I hope you got my telegram about the hotel?'

'Yes, I told Marie. She promised to arrange everything. She said she'd meet us at the Dome.'

'Oh dear! I do wish you had done it yourself. She can be terribly extravagant!' And he looked so gloomy and agitated that I began to think that it must have been the state of his finances and not his poetry reading which had preoccupied him as he left the plane.

Marie and the hotel manager were waiting for us on the steps of the Dome.

'I hope you haven't taken a room for me here?' He asked as soon as he had greeted her.

'Yes, I have. There just isn't another hotel. It's a very nice room. Come and look at it'.

'Has it got a bath?'

'Of course.'

'Then it must be very expensive.'

Reluctantly he allowed himself to be led off to the lift. The room was one of the best with a balcony overlooking the sea. He gave a quick glance round it and backed out. 'I'm afraid that's not at all what I wanted. I was thinking of something quite small without a bathroom.'

For half an hour we went from floor to floor but as all the rooms, whatever their size, had baths, none of them satisfied him. Finally, in desperation, the manager took us to a servant's attic at the back of the hotel. It was very small with an iron bedstead and a wash-handstand with enamel jug and basin. He stayed in it for several minutes while we waited in the passage. When he came out he had the same abstracted look as when he had left the aeroplane. 'It's very nice.' He broke a long silence. 'But I think I'll take the first room we looked at, after all.'

I was beginning to understand my colleagues' call for a boycott but Larry had been right. His visit was only into its first couple of hours and already I was under his spell. I would not have missed a minute of it.

Sir Eugen had scarcely settled into the Dome when he received an invitation to stay with the Governor. The political situation, not only in Cyprus but all over the Middle East, was becoming increasingly unstable. As a result the island's military installations were under review. When Sir Eugen moved into Government House one of his fellow guests was Hoare-Belisha, the Secretary of State at the War Office in whose honour a large party was to be given that evening. Apart from the top army and air force commanders and the heads of government departments, all the old diehards among the residents had been invited. At Sir Eugen's request, my name had been added to the list. He rang up to ask me to go early. There were one or two things he wanted to discuss before the party began.

When I arrived I found him alone in the large drawing-room where the reception was to be held. 'Ah, my dear fellow,' he swept down on me, 'How very good of you to be so punctual! I hope it hasn't put you out, but it occurred to me we oughtn't to let such a wonderful opportunity slip. I felt you might like to put it to the Governor that I should start the party off with a few poems.'

I had thought that after the Dome episode my loyalty to him would be rock-like, but as I imagined the reaction of those hard-faced military men and tough colonials when they found they had to listen to a poetry recital before they could get their hands on a drink, to my shame I crumbled. 'No! No!' I cried. 'I couldn't possibly suggest it! After all, you are a guest here; I think you should ask him yourself.'

'Perhaps you're right. It was just that I thought you might like to take the credit for putting the idea forward, but I quite understand that under the circumstances it might come better from me.'

At that moment Sir Robert Armitage, the Governor, came into the room.

'Ah, my dear Armitage, I was hoping to have a word with you before your guests arrived. We were just discussing (I writhed at being associated with the appalling proposal he was about to make) a little scheme of mine. I've often found from practical experience that there's no better way to start off a cocktail party than with a short poetry recital. I've made a selection,' he took a sheaf of papers out of his pocket, 'which I think you'll find very suitable in view of the presence of the Secretary of State. I've left out the 'Charge of the Light Brigade' as I thought it too hackneyed, but I've included . . .'

Sir Robert, an agreeable and intelligent man but not strong on culture, took the proposal more calmly than I had expected. 'I don't doubt it would go down very well on some occasions,' he said ignoring the papers held out towards him, 'but I don't think it would be a success this evening.' Then, turning to me, 'You know the kind of people who'll be coming. I'm sure you'd agree that they wouldn't appreciate it.'

I hesitated, conscious that if Larry were in my shoes, as a poet, he would have championed Sir Eugen to the hilt, but I was made of more cowardly stuff. 'I'm afraid you're right, sir,' I murmured feebly. 'They're not exactly poetry lovers, I should think.'

Sir Eugen looked hurt. 'Well, if that's what you both feel, I suppose I had better give up the idea but I'm sure it would have been a success.' He sadly stuffed the papers back into his pocket.

It was on the following evening that he gave his recital. Taking Larry's advice I had suggested to the headmaster of the English School that he might like to send along some of his senior boys. The school was much favoured by Cypriot parents, particularly from the country districts, who wished their sons to go into government service. The majority of the pupils were Greek but there was a fair proportion of Turks. Despite the growing political tension there had been no disturbances within the school nor had any of the Greek contingent taken part in the recent demonstrations spearheaded by children from the Greek secondary schools in Nicosia.

The audience for the recital turned out to be much bigger than I had expected, with the boys from the English School forming a solid block at the front. He had discussed his programme with me at length and I knew that the poems he had chosen were harmless, but I was not prepared for his introduction. I had told him about the English School and had perhaps misled him into assuming that all pupils were loyal subjects of the Crown. After starting off with some reminiscences of his own school days which left them baffled, he continued with a rousing 'King-and-Country, Flag-and-Commonwealth' speech which produced impatient boot-scraping and sinister mutters from the front rows. I longed to get up and beg him to stop, but fortunately he sensed the growing restiveness and cutting himself short, took off on his first poem.

I have no doubt that if he had gone on to the stage instead of into the Diplomatic Service, Sir Eugen would have been one of the great actors of his time. From first line to last the recital with its vocal inflexions and the gestures which accompanied them, held his audience, schoolboys and all, silent and amazed.

'I shot an arrow into the air . . .' As he drew one hand away from the other, you could hear the bowstring twang, and as he gazed into the distance, thrilled young faces in the front rows jerked round in the expectation of seeing some old lady at the back transfixed through an eyeball.

The final applause was so long that he gave several encores; but I had found the performance nerve-wracking and was relieved when I got him safely back to our house. After pouring him out a glass of water, which is all he would take, I helped myself to a strong whisky.

We had asked a few people in to meet him. The first guests to arrive were a leading Greek businessman with his wife, who although it was a warm evening, was wearing the fur coat she had bought that winter in London. She was rather plump and evidently feeling the heat. When I introduced her to Sir Eugen, he took a step back as if to get her properly into focus. 'What a charming lady!' He gave me an approving glance as if I had achieved a remarkable social feat in persuading her to come. 'And if you allow me to say so, what a beautiful fur! I don't think I've ever seen one like it.'

Larry, who had not turned up for the reading, arrived late. 'How are you getting on with him? He's terrific, isn't he?'

'Terrific!' I agreed. 'He's got the whole lot of them eating out of his hand.'

'He always does. That's what made the Foreign Office so mad. They thought he was making a fool of himself but, of course, when it came to it, he was more successful than any of them. All that charm and flattery from an Englishman! Foreigners can hardly believe it. In a crisis, as in the *Graf Spee battle*, they'd do anything he wanted. Of course it's all calculated. If you pull his leg about it, he calls it the "Latin-American technique".'

'When there was trouble on the British-owned railways in Argentina, he went round all the stations presenting every worker with a medal with Lord Willingdon's head on it. Heaven knows where he got them from but it must have been something to do with when Willingdon was viceroy in India. Apparently he was furious when he found out about it. Anyhow it was an enormous success. The workers forgot their grievances and settled down quite happily afterwards.'

As our guests said goodbye, repeating over and over again how delighted they were to have met such a charming and distinguished gentleman, I thought that if the governors of Cyprus had had a little more of the Latin-American technique, the Greek Cypriots might have abandoned their call for union with Greece years ago and settled for being solidly British.

The party over, we proposed taking him out to dinner. No! No! The food we had prepared with the drinks had been so delicious – 'what a treasure of a cook you must have!' – that he couldn't possibly eat another thing. As we stood stumped for what else we could offer to entertain him, having adopted his most abstracted air he came courteously out of it to our rescue. He had heard that the cabarets in Nicosia were among the best in the Middle East. Their fame had travelled even as far as Tripoli. If it would be agreeable to us and would not put us out in any way, he would be delighted to be taken to one of them.

The Nicosia cabarets must have been among the feeblest and tattiest, though not among the sleaziest, in the Middle East or indeed anywhere else in the world. What alone redeemed them was the ineptitude of the performers which often made turns intended to be taken seriously, laughable. But Larry wickedly encouraged him. 'Oh yes, they're not at all bad. The girls come from all over the place, Alexandria, Beirut, Istanbul and some even from Bucharest. They're always worth seeing.'

Thanks to the Latin-American technique our party had lasted much longer than was customary. By the time we reached the cabaret, reputedly the best in town, the performance had already begun. The audience, mostly young men, guffawed and nudged each other as they gawped at the erotic prancing of the can-can dancers whose attractions were less in their looks than in their after-the-show availability. The entry into this milieu of an elderly, grey-haired English gentleman, so exceptionally tall and of such evident distinction, turned all heads. A waiter guided us to a vacant table with the best view of the stage. We all ordered our drinks except for Sir Eugen who sat gazing entranced at the dancing girls. When I managed to distract him, he turned apologetically. 'Oh my dear fellow, you don't have to bother about me, I'll just have a glass of milk.'

I had to repeat the order twice before the waiter took it in. Mumbling that they didn't serve milk, he retired with an undertaking to speak to the manager. The manager, after repeating this negative response, offered one from a variety of soft drinks as an alternative. But Sir Eugen was not to be fobbed off with a Coca-Cola. Turning on at full strength his most persuasive charm he overwhelmed the manager with compliments ending with the suggestion that there must surely be a dairy not too far off in the neighbourhood and that in such a splendidly run establishment there must be someone who could be sent out to purchase a pint bottle.

Ten minutes later, between his murmurs of astonished appreciation of each new turn, as acrobats tottered, dancers flounced out of step and jugglers dropped their clubs, he sat serenely sipping at his glass of milk.

After his stay at Government House Sir Eugen returned to the Dome. One morning he rang me up at my office.

'My dear fellow, isn't it terrible about these floods in Australia! I felt we really had to do something to help, so I've persuaded the manager to let me have the ballroom for a reading on Sunday. I thought a selection of poems from the Commonwealth would be appropriate. We'll hand the hat round and see how much we can collect. I'm having a few people to dinner before and I'm counting on you to come.'

When I arrived at the hotel, the hall porter told me Sir Eugen wanted me to go up to his room. I found him sitting on the floor surrounded by sheets of poems in typescript through which he was frantically searching. 'I'm sorry but I'm afraid I won't be able to join you for dinner. As you see I haven't quite completed my programme yet. You'll find Marie and my other guests in the dining-room. I'll come down as soon as I've finished.'

One of the guests was his lawyer. 'Extraordinary chap, Eugen,' he murmured to me. 'I've known him all my life. He's an absolutely splendid fellow, but he's got this mania for getting up on his hind legs and spouting. Can't understand it myself, but give him the slightest chance and there's no stopping him.'

We had just finished dinner when he appeared with a wad of papers under his arm. 'I'm sorry to drag you away, but I'd be grateful if you would give me a little help with the arrangements.'

I followed him into the ballroom which had been filled with chairs some of which were already occupied by elderly residents who had come to listen to the recital. He led me on to the platform at one end and asked me to sit down at the table from which he was going to read. 'Just stay there and keep waving your arms while I get the lighting right. You see, you can make an awful fool of yourself if you throw comical shadows.'

For ten minutes I sat flinging my arms about while he circled round with a battery of reading lamps and the gathering audience gazed at me in horror. It seemed hardly fair to ask me to behave like a lunatic to save him from a laugh or two at the wrong moment, but I was now so completely captivated by him that had I been faced with the Government House situation again I would have manfully stood up for poetry before cocktails.

The recital lasted for a very long time. It started off in South Africa and moved on through the rest of the continent to Gibraltar and Malta then, skipping Cyprus, headed for the Far East touching down in Malaysia and Singapore to end up for a prolonged work-out in the Antipodes. At intervals quite irrelevant material was introduced as when with perfectly simulated astonishment he announced: 'Ah here's a poem about a dog! I can't think how it slipped in. It's got nothing to do with the Commonwealth, but I'm sure you're all dog-lovers' – (there was a shuffling and tittering in the audience which signified without it actually being said, 'How could he have guessed!') – 'so I think I'll read it just the same.'

When the hat was handed round I half expected him to cheat by putting in some notes of his own but he had no need to: the old ladies and gentlemen of the Dome had been so mesmerised by him that they stumped up over forty pounds.

On his return to Tripoli he wrote to thank me for the arrangements I had made. 'I was delighted to meet a fellow old Etonian in Cyprus,' the letter concluded, 'and I am sending you a publication of mine which I am sure you will find interesting.'

Enclosed was a pamphlet containing a list of names, including his own, of all the boys who had been at McNaughton's house at Eton. I noticed later that it featured among his publications in *Who's Who*. In the months which followed when, with the outbreak of violence on the island, bombings and shootings were increasing daily, he sent me at regular intervals letters identical with the first, dove-like reminders of more peaceful times, with copies of the house list attached.

More than ten years later, in the spring of 1965, Mrs Barnes, the secretary of the Union Belgo-Britannique, tripped into my Brussels office bubbling with excitement. She had just had a letter from Sir Eugen offering to give a poetry recital the following month. He had been a regular visitor for many years. His performances had always attracted large and enthusiastic audiences. Last year he had had to cancel. The Union's members would be delighted to hear that he had not deserted them. I, too, was delighted, the more so since the arrangements for his visit would not be mine but Mrs Barnes's responsibility.

Recalling how he had been invited to stay with the Governor in Cyprus I thought I should tell the ambassador, Sir Roderick Barclay, that he was coming. He had, after all, at the time of the sinking of the *Graf Spee* been a hero with the British public if not with the Foreign Office. I suggested to Sir Roderick that he might like to ask him to lunch. The response was a cry of alarm. 'For God's sake, don't let him near the embassy! He can be relied upon to make the most infernal nuisance of himself. The Office had it put out years ago that we shouldn't have anything to do with him.'

On the day of his arrival Mrs Barnes came to see me after meeting him at the station. As keen an admirer as I was, she cheerfully recounted how he had travelled from Paris in a reserved first-class compartment which he had filled with twelve suitcases and numerous packages. She had had trouble finding porters and there had been an angry scene outside the station when they had complained forcibly of being under-tipped. There had been problems, too, about taxis. One was immediately available but the driver refused to overburden his cab. They had had to wait for another taxi to take a second load. At the hotel the hall porters, unable to believe that so much luggage belonged to one person, had nearly sent half of it off with a group of departing Americans. But in the end all had been well and Sir Eugen, though looking a little frailer, she thought, had been as charming and courteous as ever. I had asked her to give him a note inviting him to lunch. In the reply she brought, he wrote how delighted he would have been to have accepted, but that unfortunately his visit was to be very short and he was already fully engaged. He looked forward to seeing us at his recital.

The audience was not quite as big as Mrs Barnes had predicted, but there were plenty of old faithfuls who applauded when he entered the room. I did not think he looked any frailer than when I had last seen him but, whereas before his back had been so remarkably straight, I detected the hint of an incipient stoop.

As the applause died down, standing on the dais beside the table at which he was to give his recital, smiling benignly, he made a brief, silent appraisal of the audience, then to their delight launched into a virtuoso display of the Latin-American technique. 'What a pleasure to see so many old friends! How generous of you all to have forgiven my cancellation last year for reasons, I assure you, beyond my control! How delightful to be back with you again! And who do I see there? My dear old friend baron so-and-so, and dear baroness, looking, if I may say so, younger than ever! How kind of you to have come! General, dear general! What an honour!' For a full five minutes his gaze roved over the audience until it finally settled on a large formidable-looking lady in the front row. 'And you Madame, I may be mistaken but I don't remember having the pleasure of your presence on one of these occasions before. What might your name be?' Taken aback and evidently huffed she ruffled up menacingly in her voluminous fur coat.

'Mrs Buzzard.'

Silenced for a full twenty seconds his response, when it came, was not only far from apt but lacked his usual brio.

'And a very nice name, too!'

Perhaps because he was abashed that for once his technique had let him down, his recital proved disappointingly tame and sadly short on the theatricality which had so mesmerised the boys of the English School in Nicosia. But at the end the faithful rallied loyally. As they clapped and jostled to shake his hand, he was as profligate with his compliments as ever, but I sensed it was a hollow show. With Mrs Buzzard the technique had faltered and his confidence had been shaken.

Six years later in Paris I had a flight of letters from him inviting us to a dinner party at the Ritz which he and Lady Effie were giving for a few of their Parisian friends.

On arrival at the hotel we were ushered into the large private dining-room which he had reserved. The tables were at one end, at the other about forty guests were already assembled drinking. We looked round for our host whose height had always made him stand out at any gathering, but we could not see him. Glimpsing Lady Effie at the other side of the room we edged our way towards her. We didn't see anyone we knew among the guests. The general lack of animation suggested that few of them were known to each other. Most, but not all, were elderly. There was a scattering of officers in uniform among them. Half way across the room we came across a little white-haired man who was heading in the same direction as we were, but seemed in danger of being overwhelmed by the crowd. It was only when he turned that, amazed and shocked, we realised it was Sir Eugen himself, shrunk, poor man, from a distinguished six-foot-three to what could have been little more than a diminutive five-foot-six.

'Ah my dear fellow, how pleased I am to see you! And you dear Madame, charming as ever, how kind of you to come! But what terrible news about the pound!' (Its devaluation had been announced that morning.) 'It has taken me quite by surprise. I simply don't know how I'm going to have enough money to pay for the dinner, I've had to cut down on the courses. But you must excuse me, I have to speak to the head waiter. Of course you know everyone here so I won't have to introduce you.'

As he moved away one of his guests who had overheard me talking to him introduced himself apologetically. 'I received an invitation but I have no idea why I'm here. Please could you tell me, who is this Sir Millington?'

At dinner I found myself sitting opposite Sir Eugen's daughter,

Marie, whom I had not seen since we had met in Cyprus. At that time she had been engaged to an Austrian prince, but I had heard it had come to nothing and that she had married a Sicilian duke. Although it was twenty years since I had last seen her, I recognised her at once. If she had changed it was not so much in her looks as in her loss of vitality.

Failing to make conversational progress with the ladies on either side of me, who appeared as vague about the reason for their presence as the guest who had approached me earlier, I leaned forward to remind Marie that we had met when she was having a house built for her near Kyrenia. She denied any recollection of our meeting.

'We often used to see each other with Lawrence Durrell,' I persisted. She stared blankly back. 'Surely you remember him?'

Whether she remembered or not, his name brought no reaction from her whatsoever. Mortified, I gave up. It was some consolation to observe that neither of the men sitting beside her had better luck than I had. She sat in silence throughout the dinner, her blank look becoming steadily more glazed.

The evening could hardly have been counted a success. There was then, and still may be, a convention among Parisians that guests never left a dinner party before midnight. This could result in painful *longueurs* with everyone giving surreptitious glances at their watches until at the longed-for hour all would get up simultaneously. Exclaiming that they had no idea it was so late they would thank their host and hostess and leave as hurriedly as decently possible. But on this occasion the convention was dispensed with and the gathering broke up well before midnight.

It had been a strange evening and a disturbing one. While I had only been left to wonder about Marie, I had been genuinely distressed by Sir Eugen's transformation. It was heartening, however, to learn when we said goodbye to him, that in spite of his infirmity he had not given up what his lawyer had rather unkindly described as 'his mania for getting on his hind legs and spouting'.

'I'll be seeing you again next month,' he said. 'I've been invited to give a lecture to the Cercle National des Armées. They intend arranging for some of the cadets from St-Cyr to be present. Of course, I'll make sure you get an invitation.'

He wrote soon afterwards to let me know the date of his return to Paris and the hotel at which he would be staying. On the day of his arrival I called in the evening at the hotel and found him in the lounge with Lady Effie. He appeared weak and tired. He admitted that the journey had exhausted him. He had been unwell recently but could not consider letting down the Cercle National and the cadets to whom he regarded it as a rare privilege to be invited to speak. I asked him if he was going to talk about the sinking of the *Graf Spee*. No, he'd given that one already. This was to be more personal; his own reflections on the Allied leaders and the fighting spirit of the Allied armies in the First World War. He felt it could be of value to young men who might, in these dangerous times, be called upon to play a vital role in the defence of Western Europe.

The day before he was to give his lecture I had a message from Lady Effie to say that he had been taken ill and was in the American hospital. I went to see him that afternoon. Sitting up in bed, his diminished stature no longer apparent, his handsome features enhanced by extreme pallor, illness had restored to him that air of immense distinction which had so impressed me when I had first met him at the airport in Cyprus.

To my surprise he did not seem too upset about his lecture. I think he had realised for some time that it was unlikely he would be able to give it. He was saddened, of course, but the president of the Cercle had been most kind. He had come to see him and taken away a copy of the lecture which he had promised to read to the assembled members and cadets. He was sure that I would like a copy. He took one from the table beside his bed and gave it to me. Although weak he seemed anxious to talk. I stayed on while, like Falstaff 'babbling of green fields', he recalled the marvellous times he had had in St Petersburg at the beginning of his career before the First World War, until fearing that he was over-tiring himself, I pleaded an engagement and left.

When I got home I read his lecture. I wish I still had my copy but it must have been mislaid somewhere on my travels. Recited in Sir Eugen's perfect French and accompanied by his theatrical gestures, it could well have been a stirring and, certainly, a memorable experience, especially for the young cadets in his audience. At one point I was reminded of the letters he had written to me after his visit to Cyprus, for he appeared to suggest – outdoing the Duke of Wellington – that it was not just generally on the playing fields of Eton, but by the old boys of McNaughton's house, that the First World War had been won.

I was asked by Lady Effie to read one of the lessons at his funeral service in the English church. It was the passage from the Revelation of St John ending with the words 'and God shall wipe away all tears from their eyes'. I thought that, even if they did not shed tears, there would be great sadness among Sir Eugen's many faithful admirers scattered throughout the world but more particularly in Western Europe and Latin America. For them he had been the epitome of the great English gentleman. They would remember with affection and respect his handsome looks and tall, distinguished bearing, the high drama of his lectures and recitals, but, above all, the irresistible appeal of his effusive, unflagging, and what they had mistakenly supposed to be uncalculated courtesy and charm.

Where one could be certain that no tears were shed was at the Foreign Office, which seemed rather hard when he had served it so loyally, if quixotically, from those remote, carefree days in St Petersburg for thirty odd years through to Montevideo and the battle of the River Plate.

[8]

Edward James
and the Orchid Trap

In 1958, shortly before we left England to live in Mexico, I met John
Betjeman at a lunch party in London. I had not seen him since the
first year of the war when my wife and I were sharing a house with
Paul and Margaret Nash in Oxford. He was a frequent visitor,
sometimes bringing his psychoanalyst with him. The analyst had a
red face and white moustache. He wore a cloth cap and plus-fours
and carried a walking stick. They would borrow one of our rooms
for an hour. At the end of the session Betjeman could come
bouncing down the stairs pink with excitement. 'Marvellous!' he
would exclaim. 'Quite marvellous! Right back to the pram!'

At the lunch party, when I told him we were going to Mexico, he
exploded into a similar outburst. 'Mexico! My God, you're lucky!
You'll meet Edward James!'

At the time I knew very little about Edward. I had come across a
copy of *Mount Zion*, the first collection of Betjeman's poems
which Edward had had printed on his own private printing press
while at Oxford. I knew that he had collected surrealist paintings
and had been a patron of the Russian ballet. I knew, too, that he
had married Tilly Losch, the dancer, because Paul Nash had told
me how he designed a bathroom for her in their London house.
After taking her detailed measurements he had the walls covered
with black glass into which he had inserted panels of plain mirror
at the appropriate levels to reflect in isolation the more intimate
parts of her body. Vaguely I remembered that the marriage had
ended in a scandalous divorce.

'What's he doing in Mexico?' I asked. Betjeman did not answer. His expression was blissful. Without the help of a psychoanalyst he had slipped back to his days as an undergraduate.

We crossed the Atlantic on the *Queen Mary*. After a short stay in New York we boarded the train at Grand Central which was scheduled to take us all the way via St Louis and San Antonio, Texas, to Mexico City. On our first day out we made our first Mexican acquaintance and through him had our first experience of the unexpected and odd which, in varied manifestations, including our friendship with Edward, was to become a feature of our lives once we had crossed the border.

We had spotted him at the station as a fellow passenger on the *Queen Mary*. He had been travelling first class, but ill-shaven, drably dressed and never out of his bedroom slippers, he would have been less obtrusive among the poorest immigrants. Now on entering the restaurant car for lunch, we were guided by a steward to a table at which Don Rodrigo, as he introduced himself, was sitting alone. We had not seen him talking to any other passengers on the *Queen Mary* and were surprised to find him so affable. He wanted to know all about us, our destination and what were we going to do there. We told him we expected to live in Mexico City for at least four years, and that we intended to take every chance of seeing as much as possible of the country during our stay.

'Then if you're going to be travelling around you'll have brought a gun with you.'

I explained that while we were looking forward to seeing something of Mexican wild life, we were not interested in big game or any other kind of hunting.

'Oh, I wasn't thinking of that. I meant a gun for your own protection. Ours is a very violent country. If you're not armed you could be murdered for your money, because you're a foreigner or, quite possibly, for no reason at all. I live most of the year on my ranch near St Lui Potosi. I wouldn't think of taking a step without having a revolver in my belt. When I go to the bank to fetch money to pay the peons, I always have an armed guard following me in a jeep. If I didn't I'd be sure to be ambushed on the way back. You really ought to see my ranch. You can come and stay whenever you like.'

On reaching the Mexican frontier, after the American officials had checked our passports on the train, we stopped in the no-man's-land between the two border posts. There was a lot of shouting and confusion. Suddenly, to our surprise, everyone started getting out of the train. While we were wondering what to do, Don Rodrigo came to our rescue.

'There's been a flood,' he explained. 'We have to get out and cross on foot. Another train is waiting on the other side. But you'll have to hurry. It leaves in twenty minutes.'

We got a porter to help with our luggage but were dismayed to find at least two hundred people lined up waiting to go through the Mexican customs. We dutifully joined the queue. It moved so slowly that we had given up hope of catching the train when Don Rodrigo appeared at our side.

'It's no good waiting here,' he said. 'Come with me. I'll get you through right away.'

He was a small man and up till that moment his manner had been unassuming. Now he took on an air of authority. Feeling guilty we allowed him to hustle us to the head of the queue. He murmured something to the official at the desk who immediately stamped our passports and waved us on. Once through with our luggage we turned to thank Don Rodrigo, but he was having an argument with the official. He became so heated that we half expected him to pull out his gun, when suddenly two policemen in dark glasses sprang out from behind the desk and grabbed him. The last we were to see of this kindly Mexican was a glimpse of his back view, somewhat shrunken and dejected, as he was marched away between the two policemen.

Once settled in Mexico City we asked everyone we met if they knew Edward James. No one in the circle of the British Embassy had ever heard of him, but eventually we found one or two people who claimed to have come across him in the past but thought that he no longer lived in Mexico. I began to fear that Betjeman had been mistaken and I was not to enjoy the luck which he had so much envied me.

A month or two after our arrival, my wife, returning from a women's lunch party, told me that she had sat next to a beautiful and fascinating English painter. From an early interest in surrealism, although I had not seen any of Leonora Carrington's paintings even in reproduction, I remembered that she had been one of a group of surrealists, including Max Emst, who had settled in St-Martin-d'Ardèche in the south of France before the war. As I had encountered no Betjeman-like admirer of hers in England to tell me that she was living in Mexico, I had no presentiment of how lucky we would be if we were to meet her. Now, on our first visit to her studio where we met her anarchist husband, Chiqui, to whom we became deeply attached, and were captivated by her paintings which had a magic uniquely their own, we began a friendship which was to last throughout our stay in Mexico and beyond, surviving long years in which we had no chance of seeing each other and but rarely corresponded.

Instead of the hour we had anticipated, we stayed late into the evening. Suddenly she exclaimed without reference to what we had been talking about: 'Oh, but you must meet Edward!'

'Edward?'

'Edward James. He's a marvellous person. I've just had a letter from him.'

She produced an envelope out of her bag. Opening it she took out a wad of airmail paper densely covered in spidery handwriting. Attached to it was a page torn out from *Punch*.

'He sent me this.' She handed me the paper. 'Someone's written a poem about him.'

'*To Edward James at Oxford*', I read, '*by John Betjeman*.' The eulogy, harking back to his Oxford days, ended with these lines:

> They tell me he's in Mexico
> They will not give me his address;
> But if he sees this book he'll know
> I do not value him the less,
> For Art is long and life must end
> My earlier publisher and friend.

I recalled the inspired grin which had accompanied Betjeman's enthusiasm at the lunch party and wondered if that was the moment when the idea of the poem had come to him.

'Where is he now?' I asked.

'In hospital in Guatemala.'

'Does he say what's wrong with him?'

'No, he probably just thinks he's ill.'

'Does he live here most of the time?'

'He's always moving about. He has an apartment here which I've never seen. He always stays in a hotel. Then there's his jungle ranch at a place called Xilitla. He says it's very beautiful, but I've not been there.'

I was reminded of what our friend in the train had told us of the hazards of being a ranch owner. The risk to foreign travellers of which he had also warned, had been chillingly confirmed by the numerous horror stories we had heard since our arrival.

'Isn't it rather dangerous to have a ranch in the jungle?'

'I should think so. He claims that once one of his peons tried to kill him. He's very secretive about the place. He never stays there for long. A lot of his time he spends in Hollywood. He has got a couple of houses there which he never lives in himself, but lends to friends whom he then accuses of stealing his possessions. He enjoys law suits. He has a huge house in England, too, which belonged to his family; but he hardly ever goes there, once in every two or three years at the most.'

'Does he say when he expects to be back in Mexico?'

'He's vague about it. As usual he's quarrelled with his secretary. They never last more than a few months.'

After the first evening we saw Leonora almost every day. Edward came up frequently in our conversation. Letters would arrive from him consisting of pages of complaints about his secretary or a few lines with a sheaf of poems attached. Always he wrote that he would be back soon, but months passed and he did not appear.

One day Plutarco, the manager of his ranch, turned up at Leonora's house. He had been out of touch with Edward for a long time and wanted his address. He invited Leonora to go down to the ranch with him. She went with her two boys. They returned looking slightly stunned.

'It is very beautiful and fantastic,' she reported. 'There are lots of orchids and strange birds and weird buildings.'

This sounded so like a description of one of her paintings that I was a little sceptical.

'What are the buildings for?'

'I don't know. Perhaps he intends to start some kind of colony there. It's a marvellous place. You must try to get Edward to take you to see it.'

Our curiosity still further aroused, for a week or two waiting
for his arrival became an obsession. Then we became involved in
my wife's production of *The Tempest,* for which Leonora was
designing the scenery and costumes. Tension in our own house,
which was full of seamstresses, and in Leonora's, which was full of
scenery, rose to danger point as the first night approached. It was
mid-June. Octavio Paz, an old friend of Leonora's, warned us that
it was the month in which she was always at her most difficult.
One afternoon she rang up to ask us to bring Herbert Hegel, who
was playing Caliban, to her house that evening to experiment with
his make-up. Edward would be there. He'd just arrived from
Guatemala.

Herbert brought with him the English poet, Paul Roche. We set
out together taking Herbert's costume with us. During the past
few days Leonora had become more nervous than ever and I was
full of misgivings. Herbert always brought out the more feline side
of her personality. Her reactions to Roche were unpredictable since
she had not met him; but she seldom took easily to strangers,
especially if they were English. As soon as we entered the studio I
realised that Octavio's warning and my own forebodings had been
all too justified.

The studio, draughty and comfortless as a station waiting-room
by day, was lit at night by a naked bulb of minimal voltage at one
end and, at the other, by a slightly stronger bulb encased in an
impenetrable wicker cone. Two looming granite-grey columns,
props for *The Tempest*, reaching almost to the ceiling, added a
sinister dimension to the room's habitual starkness. In a corner
beyond the columns Leonora sat, pale and tense, her hands
clutching the arms of her high-backed chair. Beside her, perched
on a stool, was a small bird-like man with a short beard. He was
talking in a high, slightly rasping voice which fitted his bird-like
appearance. As Leonora rose, greeting us with a frozen, Medusa
smile, Edward James – for this was he – rose with her, but went on
talking until he had finished his story which he clinched with a
shrill chuckle.

Introductions over, Leonora returned to her chair while the rest
of us, except for Herbert, who went into the bathroom to put on
his costume and make-up, sat down in a circle round her. I found
myself next to Edward who started telling me about his journey

from Guatemala. This had been accomplished single-handed, following a final rupture with his secretary, in the company of two parrots, a toucan, some rare Brazilian pheasants, a macaw, two marmosets and six crates of orchids. Some of the livestock were in cages and others were free to sit on his shoulders or flutter or scamper about the carriage. In the flurry of changing trains a bird would fly off into a tree or a marmoset escape on to a station roof. On one occasion the engine driver had refused to wait while the macaw was recaptured. He had already got up steam and was letting off the brakes, when Edward's shouts for him to stop were backed by a tremendous clap of thunder. With a cry of 'Brujo!' (sorcerer) the driver had quickly jammed on his brakes again.

Listening to Edward I kept an ear on Paul Roche's conversation with Leonora. Somehow he had got on to T. S. Elliot.

'Who is T. S. Elliot?' she cut in. 'I've never heard of him.'

Later I caught his last despairing effort. 'Aren't you a friend of Ann Y—? I remember her talking about you.'

'She can talk about me as much as she likes, but it doesn't mean that I know her. In fact, I certainly don't.'

Herbert came out of the bathroom with my wife who had been helping him with his make-up. He was wearing the fantastic green-spotted skin and hump-back which Leonora had designed for him. His face was made up to look as bestial as possible.

'What do you think of it?'

'Terrible.' Leonora glowered. 'It's an insult!'

Edward leant close to me. 'She's been like this all the evening. Contradicted everything I said at dinner. We'd better go before she gets any worse.'

Herbert went back into the bathroom to change. Talking to my wife Roche remarked that somebody had done something 'quite mad'. Leonora turned on him at her most ferocious.

'Mad! What do you know about madness? Do you realise I have been mad! Certified, shut up for months in asylums! My God, you wouldn't mention the word if you knew what madness was really like!'

Herbert reappeared carrying his costume and with most of the make-up removed from his face.

'Come on,' Edward whispered. With muted goodbyes we allowed him to shepherd us out of the studio and down the stairs to the street door. Once we were outside on the pavement, he stepped back. 'I shan't leave just yet,' he murmured. 'I've still got one or two poems I want to read to Leonora before I go.'

When he came to lunch with us a week later he brought with him without warning two large and very beautiful paintings by Leonora. As he had nowhere to store them, or so he claimed, it had occurred to him that we might like to hang them in our drawing-room. They were such marvellous paintings, one of a party of nuns in a sailing boat, the other of circus acrobats, that we accepted them without hesitation, though not unmindful of what Leonora had told us of how the loan of his possessions to friends often ended in litigation.

Any misgivings were forgotten when, over lunch, brilliant raconteur as he could be, he held us captivated by one highly entertaining story after another.

A week later he asked me out to dinner by myself. The restaurant he took me to was one of the best and most expensive in the city. Ordering the meal he impressed me with his generous disregard of the cost. As host he proved as entertaining as he had been as a guest. If he retold a story he had told over lunch, it was such an amusing one that I was quite happy to listen to it again. When the waiter brought the bill he put his hand in his pocket only to withdraw it with a cry of dismay.

'My dear fellow! I'm so sorry, I've forgotten my wallet!'

On my volunteering to pay, he accepted readily and was only mildly apologetic.

The next morning Leonora rang me up. 'I hear you had dinner with Edward yesterday evening. Who paid?'

'I did, he'd forgotten his wallet.'

'You are a bloody fool! If I'd known I'd have warned you. That's what he always does.'

A few weeks later, after he'd had another lunch or two at our house, he asked me to have dinner with him again. We went to the same restaurant. As before he ordered without regard to cost. When the bill arrived he went through the same charade of an unsuccessful search for his wallet. I made no offer to pay but he was undeterred.

'I'm getting so terribly forgetful, I'm afraid I must ask you to lend me some money.'

'I'm sorry, Edward, but I haven't got any.'

'No money! Are you sure? Just have a look in your wallet.'

I took it out and showed him that it was empty. I said I'd intended to go to the bank but had forgotten.

'But you can't be going round without any money on you. It's unbelievable!'

'I'm sorry, Edward, I'm afraid I can't help.'

'Then, what on earth are we to do?'

A reluctant search into another pocket produced a crumpled envelope with a few pesos in it. 'This isn't enough. Surely you must have some money on you somewhere to make it up.'

'No, Edward, it's no good, I haven't any.'

Shameless he searched again. The envelope he now pulled out was, to his ill-feigned surprise, stuffed with notes. He paid the bill and we parted amicably, but it was the last meal he invited me to.

The next time I saw him he had just returned from his ranch. There had been several casualties among his livestock. One marmoset had died from the change in altitude, the other, shortly afterwards, from grief. A Brazilian pheasant had been eaten by a fox and one of the parrots had developed a psychosis and had started pulling the feathers out of its tail. Little progress had been made with his building projects. Rats had gnawed a hole into one of the houses and eaten some important manuscripts.

I told him that after all I had heard about the ranch I would very much like to see it.

'Oh yes, you must come sometime. I'm going to England for a month or two. I'll be back in September.'

We invited him to a farewell lunch. Without consulting us, as with Leonora's pictures, he arrived with a *tejon*, a kind of anteater, as a present for our eight-year-old son. With its sharp claws and long, flicking tongue it did not look as if it was likely to make a cosy pet, but Edward assured us it was a charming creature and that we would soon become attached to it. We shut it in an upstairs room while we were having lunch. I wouldn't let Edward leave until we had had another look at it. In the short time we had left it, it had made havoc, tearing the curtains and digging a hole in the floorboards. At the sight of us it hurtled from wall to wall until with a sudden dash it was down the stairs and into the kitchen where it jumped on the table and gobbled a piece of cheese. After capturing it with difficulty we insisted on Edward taking it away with him. Once in his arms it became surprisingly docile. He left complaining that we were most un-English in our attitude to animals. I pointed out that we already had a cat, a rabbit and two parrots in the house, but he was not convinced.

He returned from England with a young nephew who was to act as his secretary. Several valuable possessions had been lost on the journey. His house in Sussex had been pillaged. An early and famous Dali had disappeared. A magnificent pair of Louis Quinze firedogs had been sold by his agent for fifteen pounds.

I asked him if he had seen John Betjeman.

'No, I had too much to do to see any of my friends. But then John still thinks of me as I was at Oxford. It would be unkind to disillusion him.'

'Are you going to the ranch?' I enquired hopefully.

'Quite soon, but I've just taken another apartment here. I have to move my things. By the way, haven't you got a rather large station-wagon? Perhaps you could help me with moving them.'

Curious to see what even Leonora had never seen, I agreed to help. We fixed a time for me to pick him up at his hotel. When I arrived I was surprised that his nephew was not with him.

'He's still in bed, I expect. Anyhow, I'd rather he didn't come. It might put ideas into his head, you never know.'

We went first to his old apartment. It was on the second floor of a small, grubby block. He opened the door but stopped me when I started to follow him in.

'It's so cluttered. There'll hardly be room for both of us. You stay here. I'll hand the things out to you and you can take them down to the car.'

Determined to see inside I insisted that we would get along faster if I helped him to sort the things out. He agreed reluctantly. 'All right, but you'll find it's in an awful mess. I haven't been near the place for months.'

The front door led into a small, dark hall. He tried the light switch but the current had been cut off. Fumbling he found the handle of an inner door. He opened it and I followed him into what had been designed as a moderate-sized living-room. The shutters were closed and it was in semi-darkness. Beneath its low ceiling the air was dry and stifling with a hint of tomb-like decay.

Edward crossed to the window and opened the shutters. Although no direct sunlight came in, the yellowish dust which furred every object in the room produced a faint, parchment-tinted glow. The space had been narrowed by deep racks placed along the walls. They were filled with canvasses, files and brown paper packages. There was hardly any furniture. More packages and several packing cases encumbered the floor.

It was only these last, Edward explained, that he wanted removed. Working in a cloud of dust we˙cleared the floor and carried everything down to the car. Before leaving the apartment, irresistibly tempted, I made a move towards the canvasses in the nearest rack. Before I could take one out, Edward grasped my arm. 'They're nothing,' he said. 'They're not worth looking at.' And he firmly guided me to the door.

On arrival at the newly rented apartment, he announced that he had forgotten the keys. With the things left in the passage outside, I took him back to his hotel. Perhaps he thought I had already seen too much, for he declined my offer to return with him. I suspected that he had not really forgotten the keys. Whatever there was or wasn't inside, he preferred that it should remain a mystery.

During the months which followed, we saw a lot of him. He was often at Leonora's studio when we went to see her and came to lunch with us almost every week. He would arrive with his parrot on his shoulder. It would interrupt the conversation with cries of 'Viva Mejico!' During lunch it made such messes on the floor that a sheet of newspaper had to be put down by his chair.

Disregarding the parrot's interjections, Edward talked endlessly on, but we soon found his repertoire was not inexhaustible. There were some stories, particularly those about his Aunt Venetia, which he told over and over again. Once he had started it was impossible to stop him. It was useless to protest: 'But,Edward, you've told us that one before.' Undeterred he would continue relentlessly, using identical words and phrases, until he ended the story with the inevitable shrill chuckle.

If he was an unstoppable bore at his not infrequent worst, obsessively secretive and unashamedly mean, why did we go on seeing him? Why did we continue inviting him to meals and rarely refuse when he invited himself, although we knew he would never invite us back? And why did Leonora, who found the long letters he wrote to her on his travels so tedious that she rarely bothered to read them, and who, having known him so long, must have suffered more than we did from stories constantly retold, tolerate his persistent and prolonged visits to her studio?

Perhaps the engine driver's alarm had been justified. Perhaps he did have a touch of the sorcerer about him, a weaver of spells which, web-like, entangled us so that, however tiresome he might be, we remained captive and ready to forgive, lured on by the ever-diminishing possibility of his coming out with some new gem of an anecdote from his sociable past or exotic revelation from his jungle travels.

On balance Betjeman had been right, we were lucky to have met Edward in Mexico, though luckier by far to have become friends with Leonora who had introduced us to him. And Edward had been right, too, not to have disillusioned his friend of Oxford days by visiting him while in England. Betjeman's recollections of the young, effervescent, open-handed millionaire undergraduate, with his ready indulgence in the outrageous and infectious zest for the fantastic, would have been sadly overlaid by an encounter with the greying, tropic-parched Edward of thirty years on, tight-fisted, waspish and, though brilliant at his best, interminably loquacious.

While it was impossible to be blind to his defects, it was not difficult to understand how his personality could have been warped by the experience of his youth. Naive and vulnerable, the too early inheritor of too vast a fortune, after a first brief flourish of generous, high-spirited extravagance, and lavish patronage, he had been befooled into an avaricious marriage. In the divorce which followed, he claimed betrayal by fickle friends who, influenced by the conventions of the day, had lent themselves as witnesses against him.

Among these was John Sutro, a pioneer British film director of the 1930s whom we met at a film festival at Acapulco. He so entertained us – he was a marvellous mimic – that we invited him to stay with us in Mexico City. As Edward had come up in our conversation and Sutro had said how much he would like to see him again, we invited Edward to lunch. He accepted, seemingly as ready as Sutro to forget the break in their relationship and its cause.

We were sitting by the fire at one end of the drawing-room when the bell rang. I went through the door at the opposite end of the room to greet Edward in the hall. For once he had come without his parrot. His beard was freshly trimmed and he had evidently taken more trouble with his appearance than usual. He thanked me for giving him the chance of meeting an old friend again. As he entered the drawing-room, Sutro rose from his chair by the fire. For a moment they stood eyeing each other down the length of the room. Whatever genial exchanges they might previously have contemplated, once they were face to face, remained unuttered. It seemed that so long as they had imagined their meeting they had only remembered the good times they had had together before the trauma of the divorce. Now the mutual hostility it had aroused came forcibly back to them. After that brief hesitation they stalked towards each other as gingerly as two hostile cats. Although they managed a handshake it was clearly not intended by either of them to mark a reconciliation. The lunch was a disaster. While we tried to keep the conversation going, Sutro, who had made us laugh so much at Acapulco, and Edward, who had often stupefied us with the spate of his table-talk, only broke their silence to bait each other with barked asides.

If Edward had been goaded into divorcing Tilly Losch, rather than letting her divorce him as the social convention of the time required, because he believed she had only married him for his money, he was equally convinced that it was because of his money that he had been thwarted in what had always been and would continue to be throughout his life his most deeply nurtured ambition: his recognition as a poet.

By the time we knew him in Mexico he had long since ceased to think of himself as a patron of the arts and regarded the pictures he still owned mainly as financial assets. He had recently sold his most important Picasso in New York and had been shocked by the amount of capital gains tax he had had to pay. While it was chiefly as an eccentric that he was to become famous in later years, he was as yet unaware of his own eccentricity and secretive about its more outlandish manifestations. But when it came to his poetry, he was as certain of his genius as he had been at Oxford when he had printed his own poems as well as Betjeman's on his private press. Whereas *Mount Zion* had launched Betjeman on a successful career, for which he always remained grateful, Edward's poems, circulated among his friends, won little acclaim. Undeterred he had continued to produce poem after poem throughout his exile in the Americas, but had failed to get any of them accepted by the publishers he had sent them to.

When I happened to mention that I had a publisher friend who was also a poet, he badgered me relentlessly until I gave in and agreed to send him a selection of his verses. His secretary delivered them in a bulky envelope which contained a score of poems and a letter seventeen pages long. The letter, instead of being a commentary on the poems as I might have expected, was mostly an attack on literary critics who could not believe that anyone who was rich could possibly be a poet. Did they know nothing of Lorenzo de' Medici? He demanded and concluded that they had probably never heard of him or his poetry. To avoid the stigma of wealth he had taken the nom de plume of Edward Silence. He begged me not to reveal his true identity to my friend, fearing that if he were remembered for anything in England, it would be for the munificent squandering of his fortune as a young man.

He was contemptuous, so he wrote, of poets who had their poems published privately in slim volumes, although he did occasionally have a poem he was particularly pleased with printed for circulation among friends in the hope of it having a better chance of survival than if left among his papers which might be lost on his travels. As for giving readings of his poetry, he remembered only too well the reactions when he had attempted it in the past: 'the atmosphere of strain, ill ease, a shifting of the feet, a hasty lighting of cigarettes, a glancing at the door and at the clock'.

Then 'suddenly last summer' he had met an American lady called Mae Babitz. 'She is pale and quite quiveringly sensitive. She was born to discover genius. Her discovery of her husband, Sol Babitz, was already quite an achievement since she came from Little Tumbleweed Fork on the border of West Arkansas and he, Sol, from Minsk. But his genius for digging up hitherto undiscovered fugues and toccatas did not suffice Mae Lou, so she discovered me.'

Her initial enthusiasm had been aroused when he had shown her a copy of his verses printed in Oxford, 'notable for having a flattering photograph on the dust cover of the author at the age of twenty-seven when he appears to have been quite disturbingly good-looking. Doubtless it was the photograph more than the poetry which first moved Mrs Babitz. Be that as it may, it was she who insisted on my giving two poetry readings in Los Angeles both of which were, to the reader's surprise, quite enormous successes.'

After this disarmingly ironical – or was it? – diversion and an alarming threat that he might repeat his Los Angeles performance in Mexico City, he returned to his attack on literary critics who believed that 'if you are born with a silver spoon in your mouth you cannot hope to hold a golden quill between your teeth'.

As I had foreseen my friend in England had no use for the selection of Edward's poems I had sent him, accusing me of wasting his time with such trash. I thought this response excessively negative as I found that, at least, some of the poems had touches of genuine poetry. Fearing that Edward might be upset by yet another rebuff and that my chance of seeing his ranch might be in jeopardy, I concocted for the silver-spooned poet a gentler, run-of-the-mill publisher's excuse for rejection.

He was so elusive and erratic in his movements I was afraid that even if he did invite me to Xilitla it would be at such short notice that I would be unable to accept. He seemed always to decide to leave on his travels as the idea struck him. Sometimes he would be away only for a day or two, as when he flew to Veracruz to water some plants ordered from England but held up in the customs. At other times he would disappear for long periods during which Leonora would receive those fat envelopes addressed in his spidery hand from almost anywhere in the world.

When he lunched with us after one of his longer absences and I happened to mention I was going to Monterrey in the north of the country by car, he at once became interested. Was I taking my station-wagon? Would I have anyone else with me? Only my driver, I said. Would I have a lot of luggage? Not much. Then why didn't I take the gulf route? I could give him a lift as far as Tamazunchale. He would arrange for Plutarco to meet us with the ranch truck and I could spend the night at Xilitla.

It was the chance I had been waiting for. Although it would involve a modification of my plans, I agreed at once. Would there be room for his nephew as well? Of course. And a few packages? Yes, but not too many and no livestock.

We agreed that I should pick him up at his hotel at eight o'clock. At six the telephone rang but stopped before I had time to reach it: I went back to bed. At half past it rang again. I guessed it must be Edward.

'I suppose you're not coming.'

'O yes, we are. I've been trying to get you for the last two hours. I'm afraid we won't be ready by eight. Do you mind if we leave at a quarter past?'

'All right, but try not to make it later than that.'

I put down the receiver wondering how he had calculated two hours before that he was going to be a quarter of an hour late and why he had bothered to ring up at six to tell me so.

I arrived at the hotel at half past eight. The only sign of Edward was a pile of suitcases and packages, labelled with his name, beside the porter's desk. I asked the porter to ring to tell him I was waiting. During the next twenty minutes more packages were brought down and added to the pile. At nine o'clock his nephew appeared, crossed the hall without seeing me and went out into the street. He had the air of a disgruntled sleepwalker. Ten minutes later Edward, himself, stepped out of the lift.

'It's all Angus's fault,' he explained. 'He didn't come in until three and refused to do his packing before he went to bed. We'll be off as soon as he comes back. I've sent him to the bank for money to pay the peons on the ranch.'

I was reminded of the dangers of which our friend in the train had warned us and wondered if Plutarco would be suitably armed. While Edward made some telephone calls, I supervised the loading of the station-wagon. His luggage included three typewriters, a rat-proof aluminium manuscript case, a sack of bird seed, a crate of orchids and a single artificial rose.

Half-an-hour later Angus returned carrying an attaché case containing several thousands of pesos in five-peso notes.

'I'll have to count them,' Edward said.

'The man in the bank counted them and I've counted them, too.'

'But I must count them, myself.'

'It'll take you hours,' I protested. 'Can't you count them in the car as we go along?'

'All right, if you insist. But if the bank's made a mistake I'll have to come back at once to take it up with them.'

'We must risk that. If we don't leave now, it'll be dark before we get to Tamazunchale.'

We set off with Edward and Angus in the back scat. I sat next to Don Rafael, my driver. Angus had packages jammed all round him, but Edward had ensured ample space for himself. He sat with the wads of notes on his knees counting in a monotonous mumble interrupted by an occasional curse when he let a note drop or lost count in the middle of a wad and had to start again.

The first stage of the journey took us to Pachuca through a flattish landscape, its contours patterned with the manguey cactus. I did not dare to speak or encourage Don Rafael or Angus to talk for fear of distracting Edward into a miscount which might convince him that he had been cheated by the bank. He was still counting when we reached the town. Remembering that he had not warned Plutarco that we were coming, he asked Don Rafael to stop at the post office so that he could send a telegram. When he got back into the car he realised that he had paid for it out of the peons' wages. Hopelessly confused he started counting again from the beginning.

Leaving the town we headed in a north-easterly direction. The landscape to our right was now backed by the still distant mountains of the western Sierra Madre. The next town was Actopan. Although I protested that we were already very late, Edward insisted on us stopping to look at the monastery. It was a handsome building with a superb barrel-vaulted refectory about eighty feet long.

'I'm copying it for my library at Xilitla,' Edward said. 'You'll see when we get there.'

Beyond Actopan we came on a roadside hotel were Edward suggested we should stop for lunch. During the meal he talked about the ranch. Most of the village people were Huesteca Indians who were very handsome, but there were also some Ottomanis who were fat and hideous. Still thinking of the money we were carrying with us, I asked if they were any less given to violence than other Mexican Indians.

'Oh, they're a little wild, of course. The first time I took the Xilitla bus I noticed a bullet hole in the windscreen. I asked the driver about it. "A fellow arrived late," he explained, "just as I was driving off, so he fired a shot to stop me. It didn't hit anyone."'

'Do they all carry guns?'

'Most of them do. There used to be an average of ten murders a year — not bad for such a small place. But there haven't been so many since the Guzman incident.'

'What was that?'

'It happened during the election before last. Enrique Guzman was one of the candidates. The village decided to vote for him. One evening they were drinking in the cantina when some started shouting that they were Enriquistas and others that they were Guzmanistas. Too drunk to realise that they were all shouting for the same candidate, they started firing their revolvers through the ceiling. The village policeman arrived to see what was going on. He poked his head through the door and spotted his cousin standing at the bar with his back towards him. He happened to be interested in getting hold of his cousin's property. Thinking he wouldn't be noticed in the confusion, he pulled out his gun and shot him dead.'

'Was he noticed?'

'Oh yes. He went to prison but got out after a year or two. Since then we've had martial law and there are soldiers stationed in the village. I've never caught sight of one, myself, but they seem to have cut down the numbers of murders.'

Lunch over, we returned to the car. Edward had left the notes stuffed casually into the briefcase. I wondered if he would start counting them again, but he left it unopened. Once we were on the road he fell asleep. Soon the landscape became more dramatic as we came closer to the mountains. A few paw-like clouds reached over between the crests ahead of us from the Gulf side. The road began to rise steeply winding through a pine forest. At a sharp bend Edward keeled over and woke up. Looking round he announced that we were almost at the top of the pass and that we were about to see one of the most splendid views in all Mexico. 'Here we are, now!'

Don Rafael swung the car round a final upward curve. The road briefly levelled out. As it dipped again we plunged into dense fog.

'That's the trouble,' Edward apologised, 'it's often like this. The clouds get piled up along the Sierra, but when it's clear you can see all the way to the coast.'

We dropped down on the other side of the pass to come out of the fog into drenching rain. The air was much hotter and the vegetation more dense and lush. Edward started pointing out some of the trees and shrubs and telling us their names.

'You see that bush beside the road there, the Indians call it *mala mujer*, bad woman. It's the nettle tree. If you get badly stung by it, it can give you a fever. There are a few on the ranch still, but we've cleared most of them away. I'm afraid there's masses of poisoned ivy.'

'What about snakes and scorpions?'

'Not many scorpions. It's too damp for them. But there are plenty of snakes, some of them fatal if they get you. We have a lot of tarantulas, of course. Only a few weeks ago an old woman got bitten badly by one. She blew up like a balloon before she died. Then there's the escorpion. It's not really a scorpion but a kind of lizard. Some people say it doesn't exist and I must admit I've never seen one. But the Indians believe in them all right. They say that if you only touch one it will kill you. A peon working on the ranch lay down on his serape for his siesta. When the others tried to wake him they found he was dead. They turned him over and there was the imprint of the creature's body seared into his back. It's corpse was squashed flat under the serape.'

When, after a long winding descent, we reached Tamazunchale, it was already dark. It was still raining as massively as ever. On the outskirts of the town we turned into the yard of a small hotel and pulled up beside the truck from the ranch. Edward led us through the rain to the shelter of a kiosk thatched with palm leaves in the middle of the yard. It was lit by a single blinking light bulb hanging from the thatch. From the back of the hotel came the chug of a generator.

As we pulled chairs up round a table at the dry centre of the kiosk, Plutarco came out of the drenching darkness to welcome us. A waiter followed him to take orders for our supper. Edward began talking to Plutarco about the affairs of the ranch; then he produced his briefcase and, together, they started on a final count.

As they counted, the rain streaming off the roof enclosed the kiosk in a solid shimmering curtain. Apart from the generator the only sound was the rush of water. I sat back watching the flurry of giant moths spinning round the bulb over our heads. The counting was interrupted while we ate our supper. Occasionally a dazed moth would spiral down to flap in and out among the dishes on the table. By the time the counting was completed, the rain had almost stopped. Now shrill squawks and chattering could be heard from the far end of the yard.

'They've quite a little zoo here,' Edward said. 'Come and have a look.'

Plutarco produced a torch. Following its beam we stepped off our concrete island and slopped through the great puddle which had formed round it. A large dog rushed out at us snarling as it floundered through the water. Muttering soothingly Edward stretched out his hand to stroke its head. It stopped snarling, wagged its tail and began to fawn on him. In the corner of the yard were some cages. The first held two parakeets which fluttered hysterically at our approach. When Edward spoke to them they returned to their perch and sat listening with their heads bent towards him. Another contained a variety of brilliantly coloured birds, all of which he was able to name. Next to them a racoon-like animal stared at us without moving. In the last cage some monkeys began leaping about and chattering when Angus went close to them. Like the dog they calmed down when Edward muttered at them through the bars.

We went back to the car and transferred the luggage to the truck. Plutarco took the driver's seat. Edward and I got in beside him. Angus was settled among the luggage in the back. We drove on down the valley, then branched off along a track into what appeared in the dark to be dense jungle. After a few miles we came to a river swollen to a torrent by the rain. A primitive raft, rough planks roped to oil drums, was drawn up against the bank. In midstream, as he pulled at the ferry rope, Plutarco told us that a nine-foot alligator had been killed nearby only a few days before. The raft sidled in the current and hit the opposite bank with a jolt. So far the surface of the track had been quite firm, but as we began to climb the ruts were so deep that an ordinary car would have been left with its wheels spinning.

'It's a pity it's dark. This is a lovely drive. A shame you can't see anything. But there are some orchids a bit further on which you simply mustn't miss.'

He picked up a torch from the shelf under the dashboard. At a turn where the track was at its steepest he told Plutarco to stop. The truck juddered and slid back several feet before the brakes held. 'Look, there they are!' Leaning out of the window he waved the torch about until its beam fell on a tree tufted with spiky grey leaves from which long stems curved down dripping with crimson flowers.

At our next stop the torch beam probed into the black maw of a cave. 'The Indians say something evil lives in there. They won't go near it at night.'

Plutarco gave a superior chuckle but seemed relieved when he was allowed to drive on.

We stopped again where rocks forming a natural bridge across the track were partially lit by the headlights. 'Pity you can't see it properly. Pure chinoiserie. The sort of thing an eighteenth-century nobleman might have had built in his park.'

Some distance on Plutarco asked Edward if we should stop at the ranch first or go straight up to the village.

'Oh, I think we should stop and have a quick look round.'

Plutarco pulled into the side. Edward got out and I followed him. It had started to rain again. The headlights showed up on both sides of the track a dense tangle of shiny leaves and rope-like creepers. Sensed rather than seen, tall trees loomed overhead. There was neither sight nor sound of human habitation.

With the beam of Edward's torch wavering ahead, I scrambled behind him up a steep bank. It was not raining hard but whenever I touched a branch, it let fall a heavy shower over my head and shoulders. The wet undergrowth soaked into my trousers and sent trickles of water into my boots. Featherweight objects tampered with my hair and tough spiders' webs crackled as I broke through them. I was about to protest that I'd had enough, when Edward stopped. The torch beam caught the shaft of a column. Tilted, it lit up an elegant lotus capital before sweeping across the front of the building which the column helped to support. For a moment it settled on the black void of a frameless window. 'That's where I'm going to live when its finished,' Edward said. As he lowered the beam something white flickered in the interior darkness.

Curious now, despite my soaking, I followed him as he plunged on into the jungle. He stopped to inspect some saplings recently planted in a clearing and a trench in which a water pipe was to be laid. Further on we came to where a wide staircase curved up into the trees. 'That's going to be the guest house. It isn't finished yet. You'll see everything better if we have the lights on.' He turned and shouted: 'Ricardo! Ricardo! Are you there? Wake up!'

There was a rustling in the bushes and a handsome drowsy-eyed Indian, white-shirted, lurched towards us out of the darkness.

'Hey, Ricardo! Are you well? Is the generator working?'

'*Si, senor.*'

'Let's have it on then.'

We followed Ricardo to a shed reeking of diesel oil. He went inside. After several loud clanks the generator chugged into action. All round us dim pinpoints of light appeared in the jungle. As they grew brighter they revealed, where the foliage was not too dense, a scattered assortment of columns, arches, moulded architraves and even the tentative beginnings of a dome.

'It seems to be working all right. You can switch it off now.'

Another clank and the chugging stopped. The lights dwindled and went out.

I had noticed all Edward's follies appeared to be roofless. On the way back to the truck, apprehensive, I asked him where we were going to sleep.

'I sleep down here when I'm by myself,' he answered, 'but we'll stay at Plutarco's tonight.'

We stopped in the village at the door of a house with a high terrace. Plutarco's wife came out to welcome us. She had prepared a meal but all I wanted was to get out of my wet clothes and sleep. A bed was made up for me on the floor of the living-room. I undressed by candle light. Edward and Plutarco came to fetch my clothes to be dried.

'Plutarco killed an escorpion in here last summer,' Edward remarked. 'One of those poisonous lizard things I was telling you about.'

'It's quite true,' Plutarco joined in; but his grin made me sceptical. 'You needn't worry, I haven't seen another one since.'

In the morning we had breakfast on the terrace. The weather had cleared overnight. The rain-washed atmosphere had left the sky at its most brilliant blue, while the jungle below us, still faintly steaming, shelved away in a variety of vivid greens. Over breakfast Edward gave us a brief history of the village.

A monastery had been founded at Xilitla soon after the Spanish conquest. At first an expedition was sent from Mexico City every few months to keep the track open through the jungle and to take supplies to the monks. Gradually the number of expeditions was reduced until a whole year passed without the monastery being visited. When a relief party was finally dispatched they found the track so overgrown that it took them weeks to clear it. On arrival at the village the party surprised the monks bathing naked in the river with the Indians. Left in isolation and believing themselves abandoned, they had taken to indulging themselves promiscuously with the village women and had been seduced into the Indians' most lurid practices and beliefs.

The party returned to the capital and reported on what they had found. Church and State washed their hands of the community and no further expeditions were sent. The jungle closed over the track and the monks were left to enjoy the carefree life they had chosen.

The village had continued to flourish until the late eighteenth century when a horde of Chichimac Indians attacked it and massacred the inhabitants. For years it remained deserted until some Huastecas moved into the area and took it over. The monastery, an impressive building from what remained of it, was burnt down in the revolution.

'I don't know whether the monks settled here for the same reason,' Edward concluded, 'but I chose it because in all my travels it was the most luxuriant, yet habitable, piece of jungle I could find.'

After breakfast we drove down to the ranch. Before Edward had bought it, it had grown coffee. I noticed a few surviving bushes beside the track. We stopped at the same place as on the previous evening. I could now see how luxuriant the jungle was with its soaring forest trees, its tangle of creepers and dense velvety undergrowth. The foliage was still glittering from the rain, but now, as we set out, Edward kept to a cleared path. The first of his buildings we came to was the house with the lotus columns. It was a tower rather than a house for the columns supported only two quite small rooms one on top of the other. A graceful but insecure-looking structure it had the appearance of being suspended among the branches which surrounded it. Huddled on the ground between the columns was a bamboo hut.

'This is where I usually stay,' Edward told me. 'I shall move in tomorrow.'

Inside, the hut consisted of one small room furnished with an iron bedstead, a chair and chest of drawers. Along the whole lengths of one wall was a broad shelf entirely covered with empty scent bottles bearing the labels of the most expensive makes: Lanvin, Chanel, Dior and the rest. A balcony, not more than a yard square, protruded from the opposite wall. On it a wooden stand supported an enamel basin. Above the basin a tap was fixed to the end of a lead pipe which slanted away into the jungle.

'I once spent six weeks lying on that bed with a broken back.'

'How did you break it?'

'I'll explain when I show you the place where it happened.'

An outside staircase curved round behind the columns to the upper stories. The slope of the hill against which the tower stood had been sliced away to allow a flat base for the columns. At the top of the first flight a door to one side opened into the lower of the two rooms. Opposite, where the hill levelled out, a path led to the domed structure I had noticed when Ricardo had started the generator.

'That's the bathroom,' Edward explained. 'The walls and the dome are going to be lined with onyx.'

I walked along the path to have a closer look at the building. In design it resembled a small Byzantine chapel. It had a sunken onyx bath in the middle of the floor. A peon was at work on the template for the dome. He was trying to coax a wooden lathe to take on the necessary curve. He pressed too hard and the lathe snapped.

I went back to the tower. Edward opened the door of his future bedroom. It was empty except for a pair of white cockatoos kept captive by wire netting stretched across the frameless window. It was one of these I must have glimpsed in the torch beam. Now they began to flutter wildly round beating against the wire.

'They're very nervous,' Edward whispered. 'We mustn't disturb them.'

We climbed the stairs to the upper room. As he opened the door the space inside was filled with a confusion of brightly plumaged little birds which hurtled chattering from wall to wall. 'This is going to be my study.' Edward pointed to a table and chair covered in droppings. 'The birds are going to be in a cage all the way round outside so that I can watch them while I am at work.'

After the tower we came to the guest house. To one side was the curving staircase I had seen lit up by Edward's torch. My impression that it only led into the trees had been correct, for as yet, there was no upper storey nor had the branches been cut back to make way for one. On the ground floor was a large open fireplace. 'Sometimes it gets quite cold in winter. This is where my guests will have to huddle to keep warm.'

As we walked on I could hear the sound of a waterfall ahead of us. Suggesting that we should go for a swim, Edward took a narrower path in the direction from which the sound was coming. The vegetation became denser and the trees taller and more lavishly festooned with creepers and tufted with orchids. Edward stopped. 'You wanted to know how my back was broken. Well, this is where it happened. I'd sacked one of my peons, I can't remember why, but he took it so badly that he decided to try to kill me. He was quite ingenious in the way he thought it out. He knew I came this way every day for a swim, so he set a trap for me. For bait he collected a rather rare orchid which only grows higher up in the mountains. He stuck it on very skilfully, so that it really looked as if it was growing, on that branch you can see over there.'

Looking in the direction in which he pointed I saw that the branch forked out from the massive trunk of a tree which was twined about and hung with a profusion of rope-thick lianas.

'There was another branch growing a few feet above it. He sawed through it so that at the slightest pull on the creeper it would fall. Knowing how keen I was on collecting orchids he reckoned I'd want to have a close look at a rare specimen which normally doesn't grow here. Of course, that's just what I did. The trap worked perfectly. As I stretched up, pushing the creepers aside to have a good look at it, the branch fell and caught me in the middle of the back. It was a pretty thick one. You can see it lying over there, but it's almost rotted away now. I can tell you, it hurt like hell. I shouted for Plutarco. He came with some peons and carried me down to the hut. The doctor was sent for. He said I was lucky to be alive. He strapped me up and told me I'd have to lie flat without moving until it mended itself. I was stuck there for six weeks as I told you.'

Walking on along the path we came to a clear, deep pool, reflecting the blue of the sky. It was fed by the waterfall which dropped in a single smoky column from a gap higher up in the forest. There were some smooth flat rocks surrounding the pool. The water was cold but invigorating. After our swim we lay down on a rock and dried ourselves in the sun.

Returning to the area of partially cleared jungle, we came to a wall about two hundred yards long with an iron-barred gate in the middle.

'There's an old woman living in the valley who likes to come up here and steal my orchids. I had to have this wall built to keep her out.' Edward took a key from his pocket and unlocked the gate. I couldn't see anything to prevent an old woman, energetic enough to come that far in search of orchids, from walking round the wall at which ever end she chose, to take her pick of what she fancied on the other side.

Edward locked the gate behind us. He told me he had collected orchids from all over Latin America. The trees were certainly full of them but very few were in flower.

'You must come back in the spring. That's when they're at their best.'

We walked on. When a bird squawked loudly in the branches above us, Edward stopped and uttered a few wheedling cries. In response a macaw with brilliant red and blue plumage glided down from a tree and settled on his shoulder. He took some bird seed out of his pocket and fed it out of his hand.

Soon we came to the first of the houses he was building on the higher level of the ranch. Their rooms were mostly empty and the jungle had already started to reclaim them. Saplings sprouted from between floorboards and creepers spiralled round bare rafters and through glassless windows. In a projected bedroom the corpse of a large bird, which had entered through a hole in the roof, lay rotting on a bedstead reduced to a ruin of rusty iron and tangled springs.

'That's typical of what happens if you go away for a week or two. Of course the peons would never think of removing it.'

He led me on, darting from building to building, deceiving himself into seeing everything as he intended it to be. He showed me rooms which scarcely existed as if they were already completed and furnished. Before a door at the end of a passage he paused to ask me if I remembered the refectory at Actopan. 'Well, here you are, this is the library.' The door opened on to an expanse of virgin jungle.

Scattered between the buildings were rose gardens run wild, huge chinoiserie birdcages from which the birds had escaped through holes in the lattice, and a number of fenced enclosures, some empty, others lodging a variety of small wild animals.

The tour had taken up most of the morning. Already it was long past the hour at which I had intended to leave. I reminded Edward that Plutarco would be waiting to drive me down to Tamazunchale. Returning by a different path we came on some peons building a wall which stretched away into the jungle without any apparent purpose. I asked him what it was for.

'I like walls,' he said.

Perhaps because I was, at that time, one of the few people he had invited to his ranch, even if the honour owed much to my station-wagon, he felt that I was now qualified to be targeted with those lengthy letters which Leonora received so regularly but did not always find the incentive to read.

The first, posted from his hotel in the city, had a sonnet enclosed with it, the final one, as he explained, of a sequel entitled, 'To the Lonely'. In the setting of the bamboo hut under the tower it imagined the poet on his deathbed, grateful to be surrounded by the 'great green gloom of the jungle' and content to have as his only companions 'the ghosts of the birds I have loved'.

I had been entertained by Edward's talk, amused by his foibles and bored by his repetitiveness, but it had never occurred to me to feel sorry for him; but then he had never shown any signs of feeling sorry for himself. Rich enough to be able to indulge his every whim, free to travel when and wherever he chose and untrammelled, it seemed, by ties of any kind, he was more credible as an object of envy than compassion.

Now, after reading the sonnet, however defective as poetry, taken with the title of the sequence to which it belonged, I found it possible to see him in a pathetic, even tragic, light. Interminably restless as the jungle birds which so captivated him, if at Xilitla he had succumbed to an urge to settle, it was hardly a promising homestead, belonging, as it did, less to the real world than that of his imagination.

But in a second letter, as always a master of self-deception he revealed himself to be engaged, as an antidote to his rootlessness and the loneliness it brought with it, in a quaint charade which, however unlikely it might have appeared, was to carry him through, as we were to witness thirty years on, into a sunset spell of patriarchal domesticity.

The letter, twenty pages long, had been posted in Puerto Vallarta, then a little-known resort on the Gulf of California. He had flown there taking Plutarco, his wife and young children with him for a holiday by the sea.

Plutarco, a Yaqui Indian, had been working in the post office in Cuernavaca when Edward had been first attracted by his charm, good looks and helpful efficiency. He had extracted him from behind the counter to take him, as his secretary, on extensive travels including a trip to England where he had introduced him to a startled Aunt Venetia who had anticipated some kind of wild man but had been enchanted by his intelligence and amiable demeanour. Not greatly gifted as a judge of character, Edward had been lucky in finding in Plutarco a reliable friend who had been consistently loyal and, as ranch manager, totally honest and devoted to his interests.

Distanced, if not estranged, from most of his surviving relatives and psychologically, after the trauma of his marriage, at an impasse to produce a family on his own account, with his habitual trick of superimposing the imagined on the real, it was clear from the letter that he had persuaded himself into counting Plutarco's children as if they were his own. That he should have gone so far in acting out this make-believe (he wrote of games on the beach, picnics and boating trips) betrayed the need he felt for, at least, some rooted relationships.

The last letter I received from him, he sent me in the autumn of 1962, the year in which we were to leave Mexico for good. As with the first it had a poem enclosed with it, but this one was printed and had a foreword by himself. Like so much of his verse it had lines which merely limped while others had the touch of real poetry. It celebrated the Mexican All Souls' Day – *el dia de los Muertos* – the day of the dead. On the title page he had written: 'From Edward with deadliest greetings'.

When I thanked him for sending me the poem, he told me that he was about to set out again on his travels. As we would be leaving very soon, ourselves, I asked him what he wanted done with the two paintings by Leonora which he had lent us; but he left without letting us know. When the time came to pack up, the best we could do was to deliver them into the care of a mutual friend. Aware of his reputation for lending his possessions to people and then accusing them of stealing them, for months afterwards I was afraid of getting a letter from him with genuinely deadly greetings; but I heard nothing and even came to miss the arrival of those bulky envelopes.

Many pages long and boring as his letters generally were, I remembered how that first evening in her studio, the arrival of one of them had prompted Leonora to exclaim: 'You must meet Edward! He's a marvellous person!'

Looking back I could agree with her. For all that was tiresome in his character as it had developed in exile after the débâcle which had ended his rapturous youth, celebrated by Betjeman, there was much that was admirable about it and, in its genuine eccentricity, endearing. Obsessively fugitive, intrepid in his jungle sorties and passionate in his feeling for beauty in nature and the wild, the picture I liked to retain of him was of a wiry, diminutive figure, distinguished in feature with his short, neat beard and, though fast greying into middle age, still nervously active and endlessly talking as he guided me on that bright tropical morning from folly to folly in his secret jungle domain.

After leaving Mexico we heard nothing of Edward until the early 1980s when he emerged from obscurity into brief stardom. The sale of his remaining surrealist paintings first drew renewed attention to him. After a journalist had visited him at the ranch and reported on its fantastic architecture, enjoying his promotion back to celebrity, he had opened it to all comers. A television film was made of it and photographs of him with his macaw on his shoulder appeared in the press. Deciding that we were lucky to have known the forgotten eccentric of his earlier years, we did not think we would go out of our way to see him again now that he had been 'discovered', but we deceived ourselves.

Driving through Sussex we came on a signpost to West Dean. This was the name of the large country house he had inherited and turned over to a trust for the encouragement of traditional crafts, a project which had disappointed him when, instead of the curiosities he had hoped for, the would-be craftsmen had turned, so he had told us, to basket-work and corn dollies. On the chance that if some of his pictures were still stored in the house, we might be allowed to see them, we turned off in the direction in which the signpost was pointing. Arriving at the gates we were told by the lodge-keeper that all the pictures had been sold except for those at Monckton, the house a few miles away which Edward had kept for himself and where, at that moment, he was staying.

At once curiosity took over. We stopped at the nearest pub and looked in vain for his telephone number in the directory. The landlord, when asked for help, implied by his manner that it was more than his reputation was worth to admit to knowing anything whatsoever about Edward, and that customers who were curious about him, were not to be encouraged. Deciding to risk calling on him without warning we set out following vague directions given us by a local drinker in the bar. Thinking ourselves lost we stopped to ask the way of a tall bearded farm labourer. He pointed along the road ahead. 'When you get to the corner take that track up into the forest. After half a mile you'll come to a gate with two eyes glaring at you. If you keep going you'll get there, but – beware! – you may never come back!'

These were so much the kind of directions which Edward himself might have given that the bearded giant might well have been one of his own employees sent on patrol to put off prying visitors. We drove on.

We were already deep into the beech forest when we came to an iron grill with large round lights blinking on each side of it. At our approach the grill smoothly opened. Beyond, as the forest grew denser, peacocks screeched from the trees and deer streaked out from the undergrowth. We came on the house so suddenly that we caught only the glimpse of its purple chimneys before the track ended in a gravel patch outside what, from its modest appearance, was probably a back or side entrance.

I got out and rang the bell. After a long wait a most unwelcoming manservant opened the door. I explained that we were friends of Mr James whom we had known in Mexico. Unimpressed he closed the door again. After another even longer pause it was flung open by a very fierce-looking young Mexican. He appeared no more convinced than the manservant by our claim to Edward's friendship. His stance was so aggressive that, with our experience of Mexico, we almost expected him to draw a gun; but Edward appeared in the passage behind him and, coming forward, greeted us with *abrazos*.

Since we had last seen him, outwardly he had been transformed. His hair was white and whereas formerly cut short, it was long and flowing. His once neat beard had flourished so abundantly that it gave him, at a glance, the look of a benign Father Christmas. Unconcerned about his appearance, he had always worn clothes that were shabby but conventional; now he had on a long, white robe (had it been red the Father Christmas effect would have been complete) which billowed so amply round him that it suggested his former spare figure might have turned robustly plump.

He led us down the passage into a kitchen with a long, central table at which he had been presiding over a family lunch. The family were all Mexican. Reminded of the seaside holiday at Puerto Vallarta I assumed, rightly as it proved, that they were Plutarco's children and grandchildren. That holiday and others which had, doubtless, followed had paid off for Edward when, at Plutarco's early death, his family had loyally acquiesced in being taken over as if his own. They were of varying ages, the eldest in his mid-twenties, the youngest, a baby in a high chair. They were seated on one side of the table with Edward's place in the middle. The remnants of the lunch were still in front of them. On the opposite side was a gathering of young people, Dutch students, so Edward told us, who had obviously not participated in the meal but appeared happy, as if in the presence of their guru, to sit listening to Edward's every word while gaping at him in amazed admiration. As he guided us to where space had been made so that we could sit next to him, stepping warily past the high chair, he murmured a warning: 'Don't touch that baby, it bites.'

If altered in appearance, in other respects he had changed little. Loquacious as ever he told story after story, the more entertaining for being new to us since they mostly concerned happenings in Mexico after we had left. His talk was quite openly directed as much at his audience on the other side of the table as at ourselves. Less nervy and waspish than in the past, he evidently enjoyed playing up to his role as a celebrity, even if it was as a protagonist of a surreal way of life and not as a poet, which had always been his ambition, that he had become famous.

Before we left he took us on a tour of the house. He pointed out the stair carpet with his wolfhound's paw marks woven into it, the wallpaper copies from a design in the Sforza castle in Milan, his bed modelled on Nelson's catafalque, the settee curved in the shape of Mae West's lips, paintings by Dali, Leonora Carrington and other surrealists, along with a whole clutter of surrealist relics jumbled, like the contents of his apartment in Mexico City, in dusty confusion. In his bedroom, a pile of old Kleenex boxes filled with English banknotes reminded me of the envelopes stuffed with Mexican pesos which he had pulled out of his pocket when I had balked at paying on a second occasion for a dinner at which I was supposed to be his guest.

Earlier I had asked him for news of Leonora. He had told me that she had moved to New York, adding as a rather casual after-thought, what I later learned to be untrue, that she was ill with cancer. Now, as we were leaving, he took me aside to tell me he was worried about his own health. The doctors had warned him to be careful. In a few weeks he was going to Switzerland for an operation.

Soon afterwards we read in the newspaper that he had died.

He had left elaborate instructions for his burial in Mexico but simpler ones if he were to die in England. These last were carried out and he was buried under a plain stone slab in the arboretum at West Dean. It was inscribed 'Edward James, poet'.

He left among his papers a vast number of poems. All his life they had been scorned by the editors he had sent them to. Ironically, it was only after his death that his most deeply felt wish was fulfilled when, for the first time since the slim volumes of Oxford days, a selection of them were published in book form. They aroused some interest, even limited acclaim, though it fell far short of recognising them as the work of the poet of genius which he had always believed himself to be.

Looking through his letters I came on his poem on the Day of the Dead. Perhaps because I had not been greatly impressed by it, I had put it away without reading the foreword he had had printed with it. Now, almost thirty years on, after reading it for the first time, I could think of no other piece of writing more evocative of the brooding melancholy of autumnal Mexico and its festival of the dead. Prefaced with a quotation, bizarre enough to have been one of his own, and written in prose more convincing as poetry than any of the verses he had sent me, it could be taken as a moving testimony to his love of the Mexican jungle, its flowers and wild life, and to his intuitive sympathy, despite the affair of the orchid trap, for its indigenous people.

EL DIA DE LOS MUERTOS

I attribute the fact that the dead are still able to trouble us to the extreme simplicity of their diet.

(Extract from the journal of Juan Cleofas Perez – inmate of the state asylum of San Luis Potosi.)

The *cempoalxochitl* meaning in the Nahuatl Indian language 'the twenty-headed flower', is the wild polyanthus marigold of the Sierra Madre mountains in the Mexican tropics . . .

On the Day of the Dead it is used extensively, to decorate graves, private altars and the images of the saints. It is tied around the gateposts of the houses, along the front yard fences or walls; and it is scattered in circles lacing cottage gardens, from whence it is supposed to keep away the Devil. Thus too at Hallowe'en the foot-paths through the forests are invariably strewn with golden petals . . .

But the days are usually clear, under a tremendous azure – stalked by slowly moving giants of castellated cloud, which blaze at sunset in violet and cinnabar reds and golds, against the enamelled silence of an almost emerald sky. It is then that the dead may seem to laugh; for skulls of pink or lilac tinted sugar are sold in the lanes, with their names in white scrolls on their foreheads: Carlos, Christomo, Hipolita and Aurora. Yet the smell of roasting chestnuts and the tolling of the convent bell combine to weave an undertone of vast melancholy – full of half stifled sighs.

On the slopes of the still virgin jungle which faces the Caribbean Sea and the Mexican Gulf, the warm lands of the Huasteca are, during this season 'of mists and mellow fruitfulness', often attended by a sudden burst of bright, sparkling weather. Coming after some weeks of wind and bluster, or after heavy October rains, this cool return of summer in a minor key is one of the most magic moments of the year.

'Indian Summer' it is sometimes named in America, or in Europe *El Verano de San Martin* – also archaically referred to in England as 'Goose Summer', because the goose is killed and festively eaten at this time. Hence the word 'gossamer', from the abundance of spider-webs seen to float across the meadows, as long as these temperate, sunlit days lend their borrowed radiance to drowsy insect, beast and bird – and summon back out of the soil the yearning Dead of every land, into that evanescence of delight, that transient whisper of re-birth.

There are spider-webs here in Mexico too, more at this season than any other. The spiders great, or small, dusky or with bodies of fire-opal, are all busy weaving shrouds. Perhaps they too feel the presence of the Dead.

The sad bird, *el pajaro viejo*, calls them – and so do the wood pigeons and the owls. The many, many moths flutter copiously at nightfall; while a bat clicks when it dives by, as though a ghost had clicked its tongue.

At noon a bee in flight gives a little scorch to the air, as it passes over the church-yard wall to swoop and sip the honey from the last yellow roses. Shadows move across the village plaza like omens of things which have already happened too often to matter much any more: poverty, illness, revolutions, famine, bereavement and, the inevitable culmination, Death. But no one seems to mind the shades of these great clouds.

Heavy dahlias nod in every little garden. The wreaths on the grey tombs are composed of aloes and cactus flowers and ferns – or gardenias of wax, for those who can afford them. The dead must feel quite pleased to be so faithfully honoured. For a spell again they are clothed with the gossamer of our thoughts; in the Huasteca now every *campo santo* burns a thousand candle-flames, day and night, and burns with the prayers of those who leave plates of food for the eternal hunger of the departed.

[9]

A Sketch of the Life of
Osbert Moore
from Tresco to Doanduwa

In the autumn of 1967 I was transferred from Belgium to Thailand. On my first weekend in Bangkok I went to look at the temples by the river in the old part of the city. In the precincts of one of them I stopped to look at a bookstall which displayed an assortment of Buddhist texts translated into numerous languages. The monk behind the counter asked me what country I came from. When I told him I was from England, he picked up one of the texts and handed it to me announcing that it was the work of an Englishman. Its title was 'Mindfulness of Breathing, a translation from the Pali canon by Nanamoli Thera'. Opening it I found on the inside cover a biographical note on the translator. 'Nanamoli Thera', I read, 'was born in England in 1905 as Osbert Moore.' The note concluded: 'His premature death in 1960 was a great loss to the Buddhist world.'

Astonished, I exclaimed that Nanamoli had been a friend of mine. The monk, hardly less surprised, told me what a great man he had been and how deeply revered for his scholarship and dedication to the monastic life. I bought the book, not in the hope of being enlightened by its contents, but because the note about its translator had revived memories of more than thirty years before when I had been an undergraduate at Oxford.

I had just finished my first year so the lunch party in London must have been in the summer vacation of 1934. William Buchan, a school friend, had a room in Elizabeth Bowen's house in Clarence Terrace. She had been intrigued by his description of

Beckley Park, a house a few miles from Oxford near the Buchans' home at Elsfield. He had arranged the invitation, in which I had been included, for her to have the chance of seeing it.

I woke with a sore throat, first symptom of an emergent cold. When I arrived at Clarence Terrace, the rain, only a few drops as yet, had already started. William had a bullnose Morris with seating for driver and passenger in front and, in the 'dicky' behind, a foldback bench open to the weather. The prospect of a fifty-mile drive in the 'dicky', if the rain were to continue, was daunting; but the pull of Beckley, although I knew it well already, was strong. Elizabeth's husband, Alan, was generous in lending me a rainproof hat and heavy raincoat.

Driving out of London the rain became more persistent. It thinned a little over the Chilterns but, as we dipped into Oxfordshire, it turned to a drenching downpour. The mile-long drive to the house, less drive than track, was full of potholes from which water splashed into the 'dicky' and seeped into my shoes. Though otherwise protected by Alan's coat and hat, I was shivering with the damp and my sore throat had developed into a head-stifling cold.

It was not the best of days for seeing Beckley but, whatever the weather, its hold over me never failed. An early sixteenth-century hunting-lodge, it had been built on the site of a medieval castle with a triple moat. Tall and narrow it had fine leaded windows with stone mullions set in walls of red brick, rose-pink in sunlight, but now turned to a darker almost purple shade by the rain. Plunging through the deluge under umbrellas we crossed the narrow bridge which arched over the moat between the drive and the house. At the front door we huddled in the porch as William tugged at the iron bell-pull. In response to a remote clang, Susan, daughter of Mrs Feilding, who owned the house, came out to welcome us and help us dispose of dripping coats and umbrellas.

The door led directly into a partially timbered, high-ceilinged hall which, with the lowering clouds outside, was deeply shadowed. It had a large, open fireplace with plain stone chimney-piece. Though midsummer, a massive log – a concession to the inclement weather – smouldered between fire-dogs on a bed of ashes. Mrs Feilding, short but foursquare and formidable, stood to one side of it.

She wore, as always, a coat and skirt of a material which closely resembled hessian, and a hat seemingly modelled on a man's bowler. Though reputed to have been a great beauty in her day, she had clearly let her looks go, particularly in regard to her teeth of which one yellowing survivor was permanently and prominently visible. The daughter of an American father and a German mother, and brought up mostly in France and Italy, she had a slight foreign accent, and there was a touch of continental formality in the manner in which she received us. It was evident, too, when she turned to introduce a tall young man who, standing in the shadows at one end of the hall, was so obscurely present that he might have been confused with the figures in the tapestry on the wall behind him. Now he stepped forward but stopped short of the circle round the fire, responding with a slight bow to her bald statement – although her guest of some years she had never been known to address him other than by his surname – 'This is Mr Moore.'

Despite the smouldering log the hall was chilly. As long as I had known the house one of the lower panels in the window on the opposite side of the room had been jammed open, as on this occasion, with a piece of antler. It was rumoured that Mrs Feilding's passion for fresh air, even in winter when the fog rolled in from the nearby Otmoor marshes, had been responsible for her husband's early decease. Still shivering from the drive, mopping a running nose and stifling sneezes, I had moved close to the fireplace both to avoid the draught from the window and to take what warmth I could from the glowing log.

Remarking on my all-too-evident condition, though not commiserating with it, Mrs Feilding stated that she had never had a cold in her life. She attributed this to her practice of keeping a clove of garlic in her shoe. If I wished to try it for myself, Mr Moore would obtain a piece for me from the kitchen. I begged her not to put him to such trouble. Fortunately, the parlourmaid entered at that moment to announce in a strong Irish brogue that lunch was ready.

The dining-room had been the original kitchen of the hunting-lodge. It had a vast open fireplace with an ancient spit with weights for turning it. The present kitchen, a cross between basement and cellar, was beneath the hall. When it flooded, as it frequently did in winter, the maid would emerge from it in white cap and apron and wearing Wellington boots which left wet footprints on the floor. Only colleens from the Irish bogs could be induced to put up with such conditions.

As we took our seats round the refectory table, Elizabeth remarked to Susan on the beauty of the needlework on the high-backed chairs. Mrs Feilding, sharp-eared, informed her that the chairs had been a present from Mr Moore. They had been in bad condition. He had embroidered the tapestry on the seats and backs himself.

'But it must have taken years!'

'No, only months,' Susan said. 'And he'd never done any embroidery before. He copied the designs from old materials and worked them straight on to the canvas.'

Elizabeth's astonishment and admiration were acknowledged by the embroiderer with a modest bow.

I remember no details of the conversation over lunch, but, as usual at Beckley, whenever a name or a date or a fact needed to be recalled or confirmed, or a divergence of views remained unresolved, Mrs Feilding would announce: 'We will ask Mr Moore. He will tell us.' And Mr Moore, hitherto silent, would provide with quiet assurance the correct answer to the question put to him or settle, rationally and beyond dispute, the controversy, however abstruse the subject.

After lunch when we had returned to the hall for coffee, Mrs Feilding announced: 'Mr Moore will now play to us on his harpsichord.'

He had bought the harpsichord – early eighteenth-century in a splendid walnut case – six months before. His friends had been astonished as he was not at all well-off and it had seemed an uncharacteristic extravagance. Besides, though known to be knowledgeable about music, he had never studied the piano or any other instrument. Confident that he could teach himself, he had learnt to play remarkably quickly and with considerable skill.

He kept the harpsichord in an oak-panelled parlour adjoining the hall. Even with the door open the music could only be remotely heard in the hall itself. But now, as if to ensure that it would be quite inaudible, as soon as he started to play, Mrs Feilding began talking very loudly and without stopping, until the piece was finished. She then coolly thanked him.

As it was no longer raining William suggested that he should take Elizabeth to see the garden. It was still gloomy and damp outside so I decided to stay by the fire. I had picked up a book to read when I was seized by yet another sneezing fit. This reminded Mrs Feilding of my reluctance to try her garlic cure-all. Insisting again, she had the maid bring me a whole garlic on a saucer. Under her instructions I removed a clove from it and put it into my shoe. It pressed uncomfortably against the sole of my foot.

Returning from the garden tour, Elizabeth exclaimed enthusiastically about the topiary work. 'Especially the bear. It must have been extremely difficult to clip it to such a realistic shape.'

Almost the whole garden was topiary, architectural or geometric in design except for the bear, which was certainly its masterpiece. It stood twelve feet high settled in a comfortable bell-shape on its haunches, its head, with ears pricked, convincingly modelled, its forepaws indicated by deftly clipped protuberances emerging from its body.

'My husband planted all the yew and box,' Mrs Feilding said, 'when we first came to live here. My son, Basil, and Mr Moore have clipped them into shapes following my husband's intentions. Mr Moore, however, is wholly responsible for the bear.'

It did not rain during the drive back to London, but by the time I reached the house at which I was staying, my cold was so much worse that I decided to go to bed. Mrs Feilding's cure-all had failed to be of any help. When I took off my shoe I removed it and threw it out of the window.

The forest began a short distance from the outskirts of Kandy. There had been a drought on the island. Although the trees still gave a welcome shade, dried-up leaves covered the path to the hermitage. I had sent a letter to the Venerable Nanyaponika but doubted whether he would have received it. Happily we found that he was expecting us. The hermitage was a simple wooden hut, but its one room resembled a scholar's study rather than a monk's cell. The walls were lined with books and there were more books among the papers on the desk from behind which he rose to greet us.

Nanyaponika was in his eighties. He had come from his native Germany to Ceylon, as it then was, as a young man drawn by his interest in Buddhism. He had joined the island monastery on the lake at Doanduwa and stayed on to become its abbot.

In 1982, the year of our visit he had been long retired to his forest hermitage where he worked with the Buddhist Society of Kandy on the publication of Buddhist texts and translations. I had corresponded with him some fifteen years earlier when I was living in Bangkok. Shortly after my arrival in the city I had become friends with a Thai publisher and owner of a bookshop specializing in books on Buddhism. When I told him I had known Nanāmoli well in his lay life, he had asked me to write an article about him for *Visaka Puja*, a Buddhist quarterly. Nanyaponika had read the article and had written to ask my advice about the publication of certain posthumous papers of the late Venerable Nanāmoli. As they were not directly concerned with Buddhism, the expense could not be met by the Buddhist Society. He wondered if I knew of any friends of Nanāmoli who might be prepared to subscribe to their publication. I gave what help I could. A year later he had sent me a copy of the papers collected under the title, *A Thinker's Notebook*.

We spent an hour with Nanyaponika. He told us, gesturing towards his desk, that he was still working on manuscripts left by Nanāmoli when he died. He extolled his exemplary life during the eleven years he had lived in the monastery and the naturalness with which he had taken to its austere simplicity. He considered him to have been, in his field, the outstanding scholar of his time. His profound knowledge of Pali, acquired only after his arrival in Ceylon, had made it possible for him to elucidate in his English translations some of the most difficult texts of the Theravada canon. His industry had been tireless, but, though producing a remarkable body of work in so short a time, the meticulousness and accuracy of his scholarship had never faltered.

He spoke, too, of his personality, of his detachment – so much at one with the teaching of the Buddha – which seemed to have been inherent in his nature; but, also, of his compassion, evident in the friendly smile he had for all who approached him. He had lent ready and effective help in practical matters when called upon and had been generous in giving advice and guidance to the younger monks in their studies.

He told us how privileged he felt to have known him (a framed photograph of Nanāmoli in his monk's robes hung on the wall opposite his desk) and how deeply he had valued his friendship and regretted his premature death. Having read my article in *Visaka Puja* he was anxious to hear anything else I could tell him of his early life.

Before leaving I asked him for an introduction to the present abbot at Doanduwa. He wrote a note but as he handed it to me he had a sudden doubt. 'I hope you haven't come out here because you intend writing a book about him. It would be very wrong not to respect his wishes.'

He picked up a copy of the *A Thinker's Notebook* and handed it to me open at the first page of the editor's preface. He had headed it with a quotation from the *Notebook* itself.

'I shall never be able to compose my biography: but let no one else have the presumption to do so; for this would amount to theft: – Don't worry, no one will think of it.'

It was ten years after our visit to Sri Lanka that I decided to write a sketch of Osbert Moore's life. He was such a remarkable man I had always felt that some account of his life should be written. This sketch falling far short of a biography could scarcely be considered disrespectful to his wishes.

For circumstances of his early years and army career I relied upon what his friend, Basil Feilding, told me in the many talks we had before he died, and the letters he wrote to Basil's sister, Susan, during the war. I had no qualifications for assessing the value of his contribution to Buddhist scholarship while at Doanduwa. For his life there I had what I learned from Nanyaponika and the monks remaining in the island monastery to draw upon, together with the further letters he wrote to Susan from the hermitage which, with the wartime letters, the Feilding family kindly lent me.

The first I heard of the Feildings, though not by name, was when staying with the Buchans, as William's guest at Elsfield. Beckley was only a few miles away. Due to some quirk in the telephone system their line frequently became crossed with that of an unknown neighbour. On picking up the receiver, they would hear a woman's voice with a foreign accent ferociously berating whoever had called her or to whom she was making a call. Though frustrated, the Buchans were intrigued. By the time I went up to Oxford a few months later, they had got to know the owner of the voice and her family and had fallen under the spell of their remote and beautiful house. It was when William took me to meet Basil Feilding in the antique shop he then owned in the Broad, that I met Bertie Moore for the first time.

Basil's maternal uncle, Christopher Brewster, had married the daughter of von Hildbrandt, the distinguished German sculptor who as a young man had bought a beautiful and extensive property in Florence within easy walking distance of the Duomo. On visits to his aunt and uncle who had inherited San Francesca, Basil developed a serious interest in painting and an enduring aspiration to become a painter himself. He also picked up enough Italian for him to choose it as his principal subject when at Oxford. Neither a gifted linguist nor dedicated scholar, he was helped in writing essays in Italian by Bertie Moore, a fellow student, who spoke and wrote the language fluently. On discovering that they had other interests in common including a predilection, amounting in Basil to a passion, for old master paintings, old furniture and, in general, antique objects remarkable for their craftsmanship, oddity or uniqueness they decided, after leaving the university to open an antique shop together in the Broad.

The two partners could hardly have been less alike in appearance, personality or background.

Basil was tall, handsome, with fair hair and a high colouring which gave him a rather bucolic look. He might have been taken for a young farmer which in a desultory way he was, living after his marriage in the home farmhouse at Beckley, keeping sheep on part of the land which went with it and letting the rest for grazing. He had had a conventional public school education but life during the holidays at Beckley with its most un-English emphasis on art and literature, and its lack, apart from a little rough shooting, of the traditional diversions and sporting amenities, was far from that of the orthodox county house. Nor did the old hunting-lodge, itself, have any affinity with the great, grey barracks of the county families; but beautiful and sequestered and filled by his parents with fine old furniture, it was to have a strong, lasting and, ultimately, restrictive hold over him. Inheriting comfortably from his father, it was for the opportunities it offered to add to its

Osbert Moore

treasures, rather than as a business venture, that he started the shop. Lacking the necessary patience and persuasiveness, he was not temperamentally equipped to be a successful dealer; but as a collector, buying on his own behalf, he was unfailingly discerning and astute. While far from being indiscriminately gregarious by nature, he had a disarmingly naive charm, and was warm and open in the company of his friends. Chronically flirtatious, his response to the presence of any pretty girl who attracted him was blatantly enthusiastic, sometimes to the chagrin of Peggy, his young and beautiful wife.

Had I the presumption of the biographer against which Bertie (the name could hardly have been less suited to him) wrote so strongly, a visit to the Scilly Isles at an early stage would have been essential, since it was there that he was brought up. That much, and most of what follows – for I never heard him, reticent in most things, speak of his early life – I learned from Basil in whom he minimally confided, and who once spent a brief holiday with him at his home on Tresco.

His father had been an explorer who was reputed to have discovered a hitherto unsuspected range of mountains in Africa. Out of prejudice against education in principle, or possibly because of financial considerations, he did not send Bertie away to be educated, leaving him to make what progress he might in the local schooling available. Whether adequately taught or not, obsessed with the pursuit of knowledge from an early age, he supplemented what he learned in the classroom by frequenting the public library where he delved into books on any subject which interested him, remembering almost every word of what he read. He had a particular gift for languages and had made such good progress in Italian and French that he managed to persuade his father to let him try for a place at Oxford. He was successful and entered as a modern languages student at Exeter College. He took up rowing and rowed for the first college eight at Henley. Perhaps because he gave up too much of his time to this activity, or because Basil distracted him from his studies by persistent demands for help with his own, when it came to a degree he obtained only a third.

It is understandable that the two should have become friends through the Italian connection, but how, living in the Scilly Isles,

Bertie had acquired the knowledge of pictures and old furniture which made him such a valuable partner in Basil's antiques enterprise, is more mysterious.

It was in the shop that I met him for the first time. Basil was discussing a newly delivered piece of furniture with Leonard Huskinson, a large and ebullient friend. Between them they seemed to be taking up most of the premises' limited space. Not until Leonard turned to ask for his opinion did I become aware of Bertie's presence, standing, as he was, silent, motionless and as much into the background as was possible. This state of withdrawal, this all-but-absence, habitual to him, arose as I was to learn, partly from shyness but also because, contemplative by nature, he felt most at ease as a detached observer of a situation or as a listener-in – rarely participating unless pressed – to a debate.

In appearance he was tall and, perhaps from rowing, gave the impression of being strongly built. His dark hair was worn rather short and tidily brushed. His complexion was pale and his mouth in repose firmly set. His eyes, thoughtful but giving little away of what he was thinking, expressed, with his overall bearing, an alert but guarded intelligence.

Now, in response to Leonard's appeal, he came forward and, bending over the piece of furniture, gave a verdict on its date and authenticity, so authoritative, if mildly expressed, that it was accepted by the others without further question. But it was not only his expert knowledge or even his rare finds, such as a Dürer drawing come by in a country cottage, but his eye for the unusual which helped to give a special character to the shop in the Broad. Objects of a mechanical nature particularly appealed to him. Among these were eighteenth-century barrel organs; for one of which (retained by Basil for his collection) he composed on a paper roll a fugue on the national anthem; and early automata, then little regarded, on which he tested his ingenuity in putting their mechanisms in order. Two such were kept at Beckley for a time while being repaired: the one a monkey shoe-black which polished another monkey's boots; the other, a clock set in an off-shore storm complete with revolving lighthouse and ships rocked by waves.

This last may have had a special appeal for him since he had a love of the sea from his island upbringing. According to Basil who had experience of it when staying with him at his family home on Tresco, it brought out an unexpected, daredevil streak in his character. In weather blustery enough to make Basil apprehensive, Bertie and his father took him for an outing in the Moore's sailing dinghy. Clear of the harbour, the sea proved to be rough and grew steadily rougher as the wind strengthened. Undeterred, with Bertie growing more exhilarated as the waves rose higher, his father – described by Basil as a 'kind of retired buccaneer' – headed the boat so far out that when they turned round, the land was only dimly in sight. But worse was to come. As they neared the harbour, the wind drove them towards some rocks. The closer they approached to disaster, the more elated Bertie became as he and his father struggled to head the boat out to sea. Their last-minute success, followed by perilous tacking to regain the harbour, left Basil severely shaken while for father and son it had evidently been no more than an invigorating and challenging adventure.

On one of his annual visits to Tresco Bertie decided, out of boredom, to try painting in oils for the first time. The subject he chose would have been daunting for most beginners but in the two canvasses he brought back with him he had succeeded in representing, with near-photographic effect, single waves at the moment of breaking.

Since becoming a partner in the shop he had lived at Beckley. When Basil married and moved to the farmhouse, he stayed on as a guest with Mrs Feilding. It was a time which he described in his one brief autobiographical note as a 'very pleasant and mainly graceful rock-pool', adding that 'the financial insecurity beginning in 1937 and the outbreak of war in 1939 silted the pool up'.

The insecurity coincided with and may have been partly caused by Mrs Feilding's death. She had made herself ill by insisting on going out in the worst of Otmoor weather to feed the numerous cats which haunted the topiary. Reluctantly forced to take to her bed and still wearing her man's bowler – for this and what follows I rely upon the account given me by her daughter, Susan – her condition so deteriorated that, despite her protests, a doctor was sent for. He diagnosed pneumonia, prescribed medicines and advised that her bedroom window, which she always kept open, should be shut. As soon as she was left alone she picked up a large book from beside her bed and hurled it at the window, breaking some of the leaded panes. The Otmoor fog, once again in its role as the angel of death, rolled in and while the family were playing cards downstairs in the hall, she died.

Her death did not have an immediate effect on Bertie's situation. For the next few months Susan, never over-anxious to rejoin Hugh, her military husband in India, divided her time between Beckley and her London flat. Although devoted to each other, Susan and Basil had very different temperaments. She lacked his easy-going charm and generally (on occasion he could be provoked into spectacularly ferocious outbursts) amiable disposition. Feline both in appearance and character, her attraction lay as much in her high intelligence as in her rather hard-featured beauty. Whereas Bertie's friendship with Basil was cemented by shared interests and mutual respect for each other's very different qualities, a relationship developed between Bertie and Susan on an intellectual level to which Basil had no pretensions.

While Susan was at Beckley, Bertie stayed on. Encouraged by her, he was no longer, as in Mrs Feilding's day, so withdrawn as to be confused with the figures in the tapestry or so restricted in conversation as to be little more than a purveyor of encyclopaedic knowledge on request. Now, in response to Susan's bright talk and that of her weekend guests,* when a subject discussed sufficiently drew him, joining in, though modest as ever, he would inadvertently astonish with the range and depth of his intellectual resources. It was the period which, on looking back, he may well have thought of as the rock-pool at its most graceful; but it did not last. When Basil decided to leave the farmhouse and move with his family into Beckley, Susan withdrew to London and Bertie departed into exile in a rented room in Oxford. The antique shop had come to an end. If his financial position had already been insecure, it must have become even more so.

While staying in Oxford some weeks later we spent an evening with him. After the surroundings he had been used to at Beckley, reduced to a small, drably-furnished room and bereft of friends to whose day-to-day company he had been accustomed for so long,

---

* One of these was the actress, Peggy Ashcroft. When I met her many years later and reminded her of Beckley, her immediate reaction was, not to speak of the uniquely beautiful house and its garden, but to ask: 'What became of that extraordinary man, Bertie Moore?'

we might have expected to find him despondent. But this was not the impression he gave. He seemed, if anything, more deeply at ease with himself, as if a restricted, solitary existence was better suited to his contemplative nature than his former life with its many distractions: the old house, and the fine things it was filled with, and the talk and comings and goings of its inmates. He made no hint of complaint about his changed circumstances and spoke of Beckley and the Feildings with affection but without nostalgia or regret.

Inevitably we discussed the ever-increasing threat of war and what we should do if it broke out. He told us that he would join the Army with the intention of staying in the ranks. We agreed that while there were obviously many other reasons for wishing to come out of it alive, it was tantalizing to think one might be denied the knowledge of what happened when it was over.

Noticing how little there was of his own in the room, apart from a few books, I asked him what he had done with all his possessions, for I had imagined that the harpsichord was not all that he owned of the many objects which he and Basil had collected and kept at Beckley. He replied that he had left the harpsichord in the Oak Room; other than that he had no possessions to bring with him, 'except these,' he added, bringing a small leather bag out of his pocket. After undoing the strings at its neck, he turned it upside down to let a miniature hoard of gold, paper-thin, medieval coins pour out on to the table in front of him.

Some months after our visit, war was declared and the rock-pool finally silted up.

Bertie joined the Army in the ranks as he had said he would, and was drafted into the anti-aircraft regiment. Finding time passed slowly beside his gun when not in action, he took to knitting stockings in elaborate patterns including, according to Basil, a pair with white rabbits round the tops. Like all recruits he had to fill in a form stating his qualifications. Naively, for he was quite happy with his gun and had no wish to be taken away from it, still less to be considered for a commission, he put down all the languages he knew, including Turkish which he had learnt out of a book before going on holiday with Susan and a party of friends. On arrival at Smyrna he had stepped off the boat speaking the language and being understood and, still more remarkable, understanding it when spoken to. Someone reading his forms at the War Office was sufficiently impressed by them to have him summoned for an interview. At the time there was a shortage of Italian-speaking officers to cope with the large number of Italian residents who had been interned. His fluency in the language, when tested, resulted in his transfer to an Intelligence Corps officer-cadet training camp in Surrey. As I happened to be an officer-cadet myself at Sandhurst, nearby, we arranged to meet for lunch at a hotel midway between the two establishments.

Officer-cadets had to put up with the indignity of wearing a forage cap, a silly enough headgear in itself, but made even sillier and more conspicuous by having a broad white band stitched round it. However jauntily I tried to wear it, it made me feel, as I noticed other cadets looked, extremely foolish.

I arrived at the hotel before Bertie. As it was a fine day I settled myself at a table in the garden. I saw him approaching before he saw me and was struck by how, doubtless without giving a thought to it, he had hit upon a way of wearing the wretched cap so that it seemed to have nothing to do with him. Instead of making him look foolish it was the cap itself which was shown up as an extraneous absurdity.

Over a rather muted lunch we exchanged news of our mutual friends, now all dispersed. He spoke little of his army life except to complain of its boredom. I felt that it had the effect of making him draw deeper into himself. It was an autumnal occasion and a melancholy one. It was several years before I was to see him again.

In February 1941 Bertie was posted as assistant intelligence officer to a large camp for Italian internees on the Isle of Man. His early letters to Susan from the island are mostly short and hastily written. He makes unfavourable comments on the islanders, the climate of perpetual rain and the Victorian architecture of the boarding houses in Douglas. Though not yet at ease and frequently overwhelmed by his work at the internment camp to which he is attached, he counts himself lucky in his superior officer, Geoffrey Dennis, whom he finds congenial and 'someone he can talk to'.

Although in his rented room in Oxford he had seemed reconciled to exile from the 'rock-pool', now so much further removed from it, he continually and urgently asks for news of his Beckley friends, is worried that he may be out of favour with Peggy and anxious about Basil who, totally unsuited by temperament to army life, is for ever having his applications for a commission turned down. Each letter ends with a plea for an early reply.

For the first few months his morale is sustained by the help he receives from his superior of whom he writes, when Dennis is summoned for consultation at the Foreign Office: 'I miss him as a friend, supporter and chief.' Towards the end of 1941 Dennis is transferred to the BBC and Bertie is promoted senior intelligence officer in his place.

Following Dennis's departure and left with no one on the island with whom he has 'the smallest inclination to associate' his letters become longer, with comments on the books he has been reading and with a growing tendency to introspection. He quotes in one letter a couplet from Pope's *Essay on Man*.

> But when his own great work is but begun
> What reason weaves by passion is undone.

He goes on: 'which brings me back to the iron-hard doctrine that unremitting self-control is the only thing that matters, plus patience, of course, and the contemplation of the virtues'.

Having arrived at such a conclusion it is not surprising that when Susan writes to ask his advice on an unsatisfactory emotional involvement, his response is a tough one which, he admits, it is unlikely that she will be able to bring herself to follow. 'I think X has taken you for granted and so is treating you rough. The only thing is to treat him rough and if he does not react he is not worth bothering about. It only needs a little strength of mind . . . I think you ought to start by having the telephone cut off.'

One of the books which has impressed him is J. W. Dunne's *The New Immortality*. 'After reading it I have become convinced of what I was already almost sure, i.e. that the infernal question of time is at the root of most of our difficulties and that it is, in fact, only by scrapping the whole idea as nothing more than a sensory illusion that we can hope, so to speak, to clear away some of the metaphorical soil and find out what the metaphysical rocks are made of.'

Later in the same letter: 'Passion and morality, right and wrong, justice and injustice are sticking in my gizzard at present, and I can't somehow hook them into the mechano-mathematical half of the scheme. It is like oil and vinegar: put them together in a bottle and shake them as you will, they will never mix, but employ the yoke of an egg and with care you have the perfect mayonnaise. The truth is I have no egg yet.'

A few months on (it is now January 1943) he reads two books about yoga, *The Inner Reality* and *The Hidden Teaching Beyond Yoga* by Paul Brunton, which he finds 'rather interesting'. Perhaps an understatement for later he writes: 'I am adopting the practice of meditation, i.e. concentration on the infinitesimal, and I find it rather absorbing. Having no one to talk to favours introspection. I have also found my appreciation of music has grown enormously. Also it is about three years since I quarrelled with anyone – this must be a record and gives me a pleasantly detached feeling.' And finally: 'I think the mayonnaise is beginning to mix, though too much oil or vinegar at once still unmixes it and one has to begin again.'

In his next letter, dated 16 February, he writes: 'I am submerged in work and have written over two hundred reports already this year. Words simply pour off my pen . . . It is sometimes rather tiring but I don't think I want to change. I have learnt more since being on this island than in the whole of the rest of my life. Study of human nature and philosophy at the same time seem to go well together and act as a counter balance.'

By the autumn, with the advance of the Allies in Italy, he is unsettled by the possibility of a transfer. Early in 1944 he is moved to Rotherham and sends a brief note to give his new address. It is the last of his letters written while still in England.

If Bertie's uprooting from the quiet haven of Beckley to become, within a few months, intelligence overseer of Italian internees on the rain-sodden Isle of Man must have been an extraordinary experience for someone of such a retiring disposition, the role in which he found himself cast on being transferred to Italy was so astonishingly improbable that he was to write of it some months later: 'If anyone seven years ago had foretold what I should be doing now, I would have dismissed it as fantasy.'

What that role was he hinted at in the first of his Italian letters written six months after the note he had sent from Rotherham. After promising to try to get news of Mrs Brewster, Susan's aunt who had stayed on in Florence during the war, he describes a meeting with an Italian saboteur: 'a most elegant young man with a black beard and singularly delicate hands'. And then later: 'I had to appear sometime ago as a witness to a spy trial and was four-and-a-half hours in the box. I was referred to as Captain X (such a thrill!) and by Italian witnesses as Captain Ics, which got trans-lated back into English as Captain Hicks.' If spy-catching was the pursuit in which he was principally involved, as subsequent refer-ences to similar trials in his letters seem to infer, what he had learned on the Isle of Man of human nature, particularly in respect of its Italian bent, must have made him a formidable operator in that murky world which he was to describe as 'resulting from the passing of armies – poverty, corruption, unscrupulous exploitation, plotting, denunciation and, worse than all, enjoyment in these things'. But however deeply he was drawn into it he never abandoned that pursuit of the elusive philosoph-ical mix, proof against 'unmaking' of which he had written while on the Isle of Man. After his reference to the spy trial he went on to describe visits to Perugia, Assisi and Gubbio, all three of which had been undamaged in the war. 'Perugia is lovely and Gubbio quite fascinating – somehow that other world which is behind the mountains or round the corner, seemed nearer in Gubbio than I have ever known it.'

In another letter a brief glimpse of Basil's partner in the Broad re-emerges when he mentions buying 'a perfectly fascinating miniature Venetian chest-of-drawers, about 1700, made entirely of glass and mirrors and glass flowers, about four inches high and on the outside looking like a piece of needlework'. But, generally, he finds little of interest in the antique shops and everything very expensive.

The longest letter of the Italian series, dated March 1945, is the only one in which he writes about himself. Looking back he considers how much his wartime experience has changed him, reflects on the extent to which he has been affected by his present work and reveals how the development of his inner life has led him through philosophical speculation to the study of mysticism.

'I have now been five years in the army. What untold and nameless horrors the word army used to raise in my mind in time gone by. My first existence came to an end with the beginning of the war. The first year served to destroy – I am beginning to realize now – all the illusions and most of the complexes to which I was previously a prey – even the inferiority complex gone – and all the constructions built on them razed as flat as Cassino. Out of the ruins has come something quite different. For the last two years I have become increasingly absorbed in philosophy and mysticism, especially the latter, the former being a kind of blueprint or map. The sensuous world is receding more and more rapidly into the background. I have the feeling of being swept down some great river in a canoe. I have no doubt that I shall end in the infinite ocean.'

Of his work: 'I am lucky in having become as detached as I am. Sometimes the world seems so universally and increasingly sinister that if it still represented reality to me, which it does not any longer, I should be swamped. As it is I can regard it quite objectively, though it occasionally requires a slight effort. Even the stinking morass of corruption, exploitation and hatred that seems to be in prospect for Europe for the next fifty years does not matter nor all the buildings and paintings and irreplaceable objects which have gone for ever. *Now* is no more than *then*. And the question of time is only due to the arbitrary order in which we look at time in sections . . . The future remains an inscrutable blank – the unreal future, that of the rest of my existence. What does it matter? I know where I am going in reality and the prospect is infinitely great.'

In June of the same year he mentions for the first time Harold Musson, an officer colleague, with whom he has become 'great friends'. 'We were together at Caserta and used to hold interminable arguments in the Mess on all sorts of subjects. The atmosphere of the H.Q. coupled with the work which, although absorbingly interesting (the three of us had the cream of the whole of Italy), was rather like living on caviar and cream which upsets the digestion and rather told on our nerves.'

This gormandizing relish, which Bertie admits to sharing with Musson and an unnamed officer, was presumably in having the pick of the big game in spy-hunting and appears at odds with what he had written in his previous letter of his detachment from the real world or, as he put it, 'the world of his existence'. Perhaps, because he had become so insulated from it in the fastness of his 'inner' reality, it was possible for him to engage with all his intellectual faculties in the 'outer' reality of the hunt without being troubled by concern for the ultimate fate of the prey when captured.

If the richness of the fare told on his nerves, he found some relief in social diversions in Rome: the hospitality of the Barberinis to whom the Brewsters were connected, a Mrs Fothergill whom he found entertaining and an acquaintanceship with Iris Origo before she left for Tuscany. These he only records in passing. More important to him was his friendship with a working-class family living in a basement flat off the via Appia Nuova, a two-mile walk from the headquarters. 'I used to go and see them fairly frequently and always received a most charming reception and was never asked for anything. How they and their like lived with the prices in the black market and often nothing to be had for ration cards, I don't know . . . I have often spent an evening with them when someone would come in with an accordion, the uncle with a guitar and another neighbour with a marvellous voice who would sing Neapolitan songs.'

Despite these distractions it appears in his later letters, particularly in one dated 13 July, that he is becoming increasingly unsettled in his work and the responsibilities it entails. In that letter, after a disparaging account of Lord Grimthorp's garden at Ravello, he mentions that he is reading 'the best treaty on Buddhism he has so far come across . . . written in Italian by a man called Evola – a remarkably clear, objective and complete exposé of the subject.' Although he does not refer to it again in subsequent letters, its influence on him must have been very strong, for it came close to bringing his army career to a disastrous end.

In November he tells of a job he has been offered by the BBC, but which he is afraid he will not be able to take as the Army is unlikely to release him. A few weeks later he confesses that he finds his nerves on edge: 'I am beginning to feel strongly that I have had enough of intelligence and never want to hear the word *secret* again.'

His final letter from Italy, the only one undated, was probably written early in 1946. 'I am having a frightful time just now . . . my responsibilities seem to grow in the most appalling fashion.' And at the end after mentioning visits to the opera: 'Without some sort of distraction of this kind I think I would go wild in the present state of things as they affect me.'

For what happened in the period between this letter and a card, dated 9 May, posted from London and giving the time of his arrival by train to spend a weekend in the country with Susan who was by then living at Stanton with her husband, Hugh, I have only Basil's account to go on. He assured me that he had had it from Bertie himself.

After reading Evola's book, *The Doctrine of Awakening*, his attraction to Buddhism became so strong that it brought the two realities, of which he had previously written that he could keep them detached the one from the other, into a contention which, while continuing in his work, he found it impossible to resolve. The successful hunting down of spies, ending, as it usually did, with their execution, could not be reconciled, as he was now forced to accept, with the Buddha's teaching on the sanctity of life, not only human but in all its forms. (A few years later in coping with poisonous snakes in the compound at Doanduwa, rather than killing them, he practised luring them into jars so that they could be removed unharmed out of danger to the community.) In the dilemma in which he now found himself, he asked to be relieved of his counter-espionage duties and followed this up with a refusal to divulge evidence, known only to him, with regard to investigations already in hand. The situation, it must be admitted, was not without a touch of black comedy and cynics might see in his conduct a gamble which paid off. Gamble or not it required courage, for it could have easily led to a court martial and a harsh sentence. According to Basil, for some time this was a real possibility; but either by a fortunate coincidence or due to manipulations by superiors well-disposed towards him and convinced of his sincerity, his release requested by the BBC was granted and he was allowed to leave for London to take up his appointment in the Italian section.

Like the card of 9 May the letters Bertie wrote to Susan while he was working at the BBC refer mostly to weekends spent at Stanton or arrangements for meetings in London. Curiously there is no mention of Harold Musson in the earlier letters although his release from the army must have followed soon after his own since already by March 1947 he was writing from the flat they were sharing in St George's Terrace. It is only in letters written over a year later that Musson's name appears and then in a context which implies that he and Susan were not on good terms.

Certainly the Feildings were unfavourably impressed by him when Bertie took him on a visit to Beckley. Asked many years later what he was like, they described him as a 'poseur', 'precious', 'an Oscar Wilde-like character wearing a cloak'. So portrayed it is difficult to conceive of him as the dedicated convert to Buddhism he proved to be, still less to imagine as remotely possible the circumstances of his death.

There are some references in the letters to new friends he had made through Susan and to colleagues at work, but none to the progress of his 'inner life' which had been such a recurring theme in those written from the Isle of Man and Italy. On the direction in which it was taking him he appears to have kept her in the dark almost to the very last.

A few months after our arrival in Milan in 1948 the director of the Italian section of the BBC called to see me. After introducing himself he said that he believed that I was a friend of his assistant, Osbert Moore.

I shook my head, 'I'm sorry there must be some mistake. I don't remember knowing anyone of that name.'

'But he told me himself that he knew you well when he was living near Oxford.'

'Oh, you must mean Bertie! I had no idea his name was Osbert. It sounds too pretentious – not like him at all. How is he? What's he doing?'

'He's fine. He works with me. He's incredibly efficient. I don't know what I'd do without him. I certainly wouldn't have been able to come out here if I hadn't known everything would be all right in the office so long as he was in charge. He intends taking a holiday in Italy later after meeting with the broadcasting people in Rome. He hopes to have the chance of seeing you.'

I wrote to Bertie inviting him to stay. He accepted and spent two nights with us on his way back from Rome, before setting out on what he described as 'a jaunt through northern Italy'. We were still living at Gernetto which with all its attractions had the disadvantage of the early start I had to make to reach my office on time and my frequent late return in the evening. Accordingly I saw less of Bertie than Leonora did but we both agreed that though his personality seemed little changed, he had become more self-assured, less withdrawn and more open in conversation. He had always been given to silences which, for our part, we had never found disconcerting. Now, Leonora reported, they had taken on a new dimension. Whereas before, apparently no more than a refuge from being drawn into talk for its own sake or in which he had no inclination to take part, they were longer and deeply meditative, producing, as she found when sitting in the same room with him, a benign and restful atmosphere.

He spoke little of his wartime experiences other than to tell us that he had spent some years with Italian internees on the Isle of Man before being transferred, following the Allies' advance, to the headquarters at Caserta in southern Italy. He had even less to say about his work with the BBC although it was for talks in Rome at the state and Vatican radio stations that he had come out. We discussed Italian politics in which he was still interested from his time in intelligence at Caserta. Possibly from what he had then learnt of disreputable intrigues at the papacy, he had acquired a dislike of the Catholic church which he expressed with uncharacteristic vehemence.

Before his arrival we had been counting on him, with his encyclopaedic knowledge, to tell us the names of various trees in the park with which we were unfamiliar. He did not disappoint us: not merely identifying them and describing their various characteristics but naming the countries to which they were native.

During his visit he had worn the same quietly respectable suit and shirt with collar and tie. But he surprised me on the morning of his departure by appearing in khaki shirt and shorts, heavy boots and carrying a rucksack. It was an outfit which, at that time in Italy, anyone who had given more thought to his appearance than Bertie would have been deterred from wearing as too embarrassingly conspicuous. I drove him into Milan and dropped him at the foot of the flight of steps leading up to the railway station. As with his rucksack on his back he climbed the steps, people turned to stare at him, finding him, as was plain from their looks, a target for ridicule. At the top he turned and waved. I waved back. It was the last time I was to see him.

In the early autumn of the same year (1948) I had a second visit from the BBC director. As our discussions were inconclusive he decided to call on me again on his way back from Rome. When the time passed and I heard nothing from him, I assumed he had changed his mind. It was not until a month later that he wrote to me with an apology and an explanation.

While he was in Rome he had had a message to say that Bertie had resigned from his post. He had given no hint of his intention, although at least one member of the staff was a close friend. He had simply left a note on his desk saying that he was resigning forthwith and would not be coming back to the office. The director had had to cut short his stay in Rome. On his return to London he learned that Bertie had already left for Ceylon, apparently with the aim of becoming a Buddhist monk.

It appears that on one of Bertie's visits to Stanton in August he told Susan for the first time that he was considering giving up his post at the BBC to leave with Musson to study Buddhism in Ceylon. Writing later in the month from Holland where he is on holiday, he starts by thanking her for having him to stay: 'If life was like all weekends at Stanton there would be no need to consider mirages in the East! Your disapproval of my proposal is much appreciated – very much so. There is only one thing I would say at this moment which is that there is no question of choosing between friends. If I went to Ceylon with Harold Musson in order to study and, maybe, practise Buddhism, it would be merely that, having decided to go, there is no point in travelling alone (at least to start with) if you can travel in company.'

In disapproving of his project Susan may have revealed her resentment at his closeness to Musson. In the months before the war when they had been together at Beckley, she had been the dominant personality, appreciative of Bertie's remarkable gifts and intent upon drawing him out from the diffidence he was only fully to shake off in the course of his army career. Now they were on equal terms and while she may have felt rejected when he told her of his intention to leave with Musson, for his part, however much he valued and continued to value her friendship, the loyalty she might have expected of him, would have been counter to the practice of non-attachment in which he had schooled himself in Italy and which had been reinforced by his study of Buddhism.

Of his final decision to leave with Musson, despite her disapproval, she responded generously when he turned to her for help in the disposal of his possessions, agreeing to take on the responsibility of power-of-attorney on his behalf. With his farewell letter he sent her a meticulous inventory of the contents of his flat with details of what was to be sold, including his harpsichord, and what given away and to whom. The letter, dated 14 October, concludes: 'I am eternally grateful to you for your help and understanding in all this and I know of no one else to whom I could turn under the circumstances who would have the comprehension and sympathy that you have. Thank you for everything. My best love to Hugh, yours Bertie.'

The letter which began with the heading 'Business First', ended with a postscript giving the address of his bank in London and that of the Chartered Bank in Ceylon to which letters could be forwarded.

Susan was not alone among Bertie's close friends to be dismayed by his departure. Geoffrey Dennis, who had been so helpful to him in his early days on the Isle of Man and responsible for his appointment to the BBC, was deeply wounded, the more so because he had known nothing of Bertie's immediate intentions until he read the letter of resignation left on his desk. Unaware that Musson had also departed for Ceylon, he wrote to him at St George's Terrace. The letter was kept by Susan among her letters from Bertie.

'My dear Musson, This sudden departure of Osbert's without notice, throwing up everything, has surprised and moved me. With yourself, I was by far his most intimate friend and although I knew that this kind of thing was working in him, I had no sort of notion that it would be so soon or so sudden. It is a terrible blow to me . . . but, quite likely, [scored out] he had done the right thing.'

The letter goes on to ask when it would be convenient for him to call at the flat to collect some of his possessions left there. It is signed, 'G. Dennis'.

It would seem from the formality of his signature and his addressing Musson by his surname that, although they must have met frequently at the flat, they can hardly have been on the friendliest terms. Perhaps he had reacted to him as the Feildings had done, and like Susan, had resented his closeness to Bertie.

If both Susan and Dennis had become emotionally attached to Bertie, even jealously so, it was doubtless because of the extent to which they had come to value the stimulus of his remarkable intellect and the humanity underlying his reserve. On his side, beyond this, he could offer no more than friendliness and understanding. Early on he appears to have set himself against emotional involvement (even at Beckley he had had a touch of the monk about him), dedicating his life to that iron-hard doctrine of unremitting self-control, advocated, as already quoted, in one of his letters from the Isle of Man: a doctrine so in tune with the teaching of the Buddha, that he might be seen to have been well on his way to becoming a Buddhist before his discovery of Buddhism.

Bertie's relations with Musson appear to have been singularly cerebral from the start, originating, as described by himself, in their interminable arguments in the mess at Caserta 'of the kind that never get anywhere, such as trying to prove by logical deduction that music must be literature, etc., etc.'

Their shared interest in Buddhism must have drawn them intellectually closer and was, doubtless, the subject of discussions at St George's Terrace which, if no less interminable than those at Caserta, instead of getting nowhere, led to their decision to leave for Ceylon. Once there, they hoped to join a monastic settlement in which, as they had learned, there were a number of European monks.

The first of Bertie's letters to Susan from Sri Lanka was written after he had been living for seven weeks on the island. He has read no newspapers since his arrival and intends to give up reading them for good. Although he had planned to 'retire into the unknown and stay there', he feels that after all the trouble he has put Susan to, he owes her a letter. But clearly he is finding it difficult to cut himself off from the past, for he adds a postscript: 'Do write whenever you feel inclined and no matter what it is about.' All twenty-two letters which were to follow contained similar pleas.

There was, of course, nothing discreditable, in his failure to make the clean break he had intended, though surprising, perhaps, given the resolution he had shown in giving up his post at the BBC and abandoning friends of a lifetime. It was, however, a little disconcerting to find in his next letter an admission that 'to study and possibly practice Buddhism', as he had claimed, was not the sole motive for his decision to leave for Ceylon.

Susan had written to tell him of the death of an old aunt whom he had been helping to support. This leads him to write of the family fortune squandered by his grandfather and father. 'I used, years ago, to feel this rather, but now, as this has been a contributing (though by no means prime) cause of my coming here, I am more than glad of it as it helped to push me into the hermit life which, in the right circumstances, is the life I have always wanted to lead.'

There follow instructions about the disposal of his remaining possessions. 'Their smallness being mainly due to the support of aged relatives whose income seemed to get smaller as the cost of living and taxes got bigger. Had I, for example, remained at the BBC I might have hoped to get back to where I was before the war by the time I was sixty. What a prospect!'

Later, in the same letter, he writes: 'I have no regrets for leaving England. I had, however, expected regrets from separation from one's friends, but have been surprised at their strength. The fact probably shows the danger to myself of declining into an impecunious old bore depending for moral support on the long suffering of others. Old, hungry and querulous . . . a prospect both unattractive and unbecoming. Besides there are positive reasons for wanting to be a hermit.'

The island hermitage at Doanduwa, where he is already living, though not yet as a monk, appears from his description which follows, with its rich jungle vegetation and abundant bird, animal and reptile life, a beautiful, exotic if not altogether peaceable place to retire to, and certainly far removed from the comfortless caves in rocky and desert landscapes often associated with hermit dwellings.

'The hermitage really consists of two islands joined by a causeway. Polasduwa (coconut tree island) has been the hermitage since before the First World War, whilst Madiduwa (round island) was a cinnamon garden which was given to the hermitage by the owner.

'The original hermitage is covered with a forest jungle of mangroves, palms, creepers and whatnot amongst which are seven isolated "houses" (one room each) and a refectory. Madiduwa is more open and covered with cinnamon bushes and coconut palms. Both are surrounded and the causeway arched over with a narrow belt of mangroves . . . The lake is large, about two-and-a-half miles across and brackish as it connects with the sea. It is entirely surrounded by hillocks covered with coconut palms. A huge colony of cranes which spend the night feeding in the countryside among the rice fields, roost by day and squawk in the island mangroves. Iguanas wander among the bushes, some three feet long and oddly prehistoric-looking, whilst similar looking water lizards swim in the lake. Large birds whoop and shriek and small birds sing rather saccharine and sentimental songs – often, indeed, tunes rather than songs. Drums beat for long periods from many places on the mainland, sometimes all night and sometimes all day, with complicated rhythms. All day from the nearest mainland comes the monotonous pounding of coconut husks being beaten into fibre.

'The weather is always summer. The sun is now overhead. It is apt to be very heavy at midday but there are always clouds about and the sky looks absurdly English. Often it rains, and what rain! Clouds pile up with thunder and lightning. Then you hear a strange roaring like a waterfall across the lake and soon the rain bursts on the island with astonishing violence.

'The day, at present, is spent like this: I aim to get up at four and meditate till about seven. Then sweep the room (the only manual work allowed to monks) and make tea in the kitchen. Breakfast arrives brought by one of the four lay attendants. It consists of rice gruel made with coconut milk, rice cakes with spiced sauce, sweets and bananas and papaws. I spend the morning between learning Pali, meditation or cooking. Sometimes food is brought and sometimes not, in which case I cook it from supplies I keep in hand.

'In the afternoon one sleeps for a bit, bathes in the lake and meditates afterwards. At seven or so there is tea in the refectory for anyone who wants to go there. Here one has cups of tea and lemon and talks of doctrine with the monks, or Pali discourses are recited. It is dark at this time and the refectory is open on two sides to the air. Strangely when the doctrine is discussed or Pali recited, large toads come out on to the floor to listen, their large golden eyes unblinking. When it is over they go away. The atmosphere is almost

Franciscan, especially when the rain roars so loud that you have to shout to be heard and the feeble light of naked oil wicks is drowned by the almost continuous blue lightning accompanied by the crashing of thunder – or again on one of those incredibly grandiose nights of the full moon when soft strong light streams down through the dense trees.

'One goes to bed at about ten. As you see one does not eat after midday, a habit which I have taken to kindly. I sleep on a board with a thin mattress which is also reasonable as I have always liked hard beds . . .

'Two things impress me about the monks here, Sinhalese, German and Burmese, – that is their extraordinary kindness, solicitude and cheerfulness and that there are no subjects which are taboo for discussion or anything which you have to take on trust.'

Towards the end of the letter he writes that he and Musson have decided to join the order, the first of the two prescribed initiation ceremonies to be held within a few weeks.

For the next eleven years of his life at the hermitage, interrupted only by occasional visits to other monastic settlements and by some quite protracted pilgrimages to Buddhist sanctuaries particularly venerated by the Sinhalese, he was to follow the routine already described. He had found 'the hermit's life under the right circumstances' which he had been looking for, but the circumstances were such and so far from solitary, that as a hermit's life, strictly speaking, it hardly qualified. Despite its name the island hermitage was, in fact, a small monastic community much revered for its strict adherence to Buddhist doctrine. From his own account it had many visitors including lay supporters, Sinhalese dignitaries, both religious and political, foreign monks, especially Burmese, and world-travelling seekers after truth some of whose eccentricities he gently derides. He does, however, in the interest of his own seclusion, make the path of some twenty yards or so from the refectory to his hut sufficiently maze-like to deter all but the most persistent of unsolicited intruders.

I had supposed from his growing interest in mysticism through which he had come to see philosophy as only 'a map or blueprint' that he had decided that it was as a Buddhist monk that he might best pursue his cultivation of that 'inner reality' of which he had written while in Italy, that he knew where it was leading him and that 'the prospect was infinitely great'.

At the time when I had first heard of his departure for Ceylon I had little knowledge of Buddhism beyond what I had read in Alexandra David-Neale's intriguing but unreliable account in her book *With Mystics and Magicians in Tibet*. Unaware of the existence of different sects I had assumed that mysticism played an accepted role in Buddhist practice. I did not realize that the Theravada sect to which the Sinhalese adhered, was so different from the Mahayana sect of which the Tibetans were followers. Nanãmoli, as he must now properly be named, describes the difference in two of his early letters.

He begins by answering a question of Susan's about Pali.

'It is a dead Indo-European language and a sort of dialect of Sanskrit . . . in which the Theravada canonical texts (the oldest Buddhist texts) are written. It has no alphabet of its own but is written with mainly Sinhalese, Burmese, Siamese, Sanskrit, Cambodian and, now, Latin characters.* It was brought to Ceylon from India by the son of the Emperor Asoka and later spread to Burma, Siam and Cambodia. Mahayana Buddhism, which has Sanskrit texts, is found in Tibet, Nepal, China and Japan.

'As to the origin of the terms Mahayana and Hinyana (Theravada) in the former the doctrine of how to act to reach Nirvana became overshadowed by a fantastic theology . . . while the aim was to become an Araket, or one who attained Nirvana while still alive, became overshadowed by the idea of the Bodisattva, or one who has reached the point at which Nirvana is attainable and who renounces it to remain in the world until all other beings have been "saved" . . . This northern Buddhism styled itself Mahayana, or the "greater vehicle" and invented the name Hinyana, or the "Lower Vehicle" for the southern form according to which no one gets to Nirvana unless they do something about it, and which holds that one should go straight ahead and not bother about anything or anyone . . . the object of living a monk's life here is to practise renunciation and meditation in order to get out of the endless round of becoming and making some headway towards Nirvana . . . good works, it is held, are all very well but

---

* He mastered the first four of these before beginning his translations.

are best practised by laymen who are better fitted to perform them
. . . this seems sensible.'

Sensible it may well seem to one who, without taking any irrevocable vows, has renounced all worldly possessions to adhere
to the strict rules of the monastic life with the sole object of
attaining to his own salvation; but to Westerners it must
inevitably appear coldly self-centred and lacking in obligation to
the rest of humanity.

This, however, is not at all how the monks are seen by the
Buddhist laity. By a tradition which may have been eroded in
recent years by Western influence or the conduct of hostile political regimes, the monasteries are regarded as centres of exemplary
living in accordance with the precepts laid down by the Buddha,
thereby extending a benign influence among the community as a
whole, and offering the devout the opportunity of gaining merit
by supporting them with food and other necessities: the more
dedicated the monks, the greater the merit gained.

Now in choosing to join a Theravada order Nanãmoli had
turned away from the mysticism to which he had been drawn
while in Italy, since the southern sect, though it may count some
locally accepted 'saints', has given little encouragement to mystics,
but it was as a mystic, retired to some remote mountain cave,
reaching out, through the rigours of renunciation and intense
spiritual exercise, to that other world which he had once glimpsed
in Gubbio, that it had been tempting to imagine, on hearing of his
exodus to the East, as a fittingly outlandish destiny for the gentle,
withdrawn and slightly mysterious Bertie of the Beckley years.
And yet it seems odd that he should have recommended Susan to
read, for her better understanding of Buddhism, the life of Mila
Repa ('for atmosphere', he suggests), the great Tibetan mystic
who after starting life as a highly accomplished and homicidal
magician, ended after a harsh and exacting penance, as a saintly
poet–monk whose life was so austere that, existing only on grass,
his emaciated body turned green.

It must be said from his own description of it, the island
hermitage, so far as atmosphere went, bore little resemblance to
Mila Repa's cave, which is still a centre of devout pilgrimage and
has about it a remarkable aura of sanctity.

But the hermitage, aside from providing an agreeable if frugal retreat for the practice of renunciation and meditation, had much else to offer, not least the friendly cheerfulness of the monks and their readiness to give advice and discuss points of doctrine with lay visitors and supporters.

Some months after he had settled on the island, he joined a five-day excursion to visit the ruins of a monastic centre in the jungle dating from the first century, but abandoned in 1400. It is typical of numerous such excursions, or pilgrimages, he was to undertake during the years to come. Though some were more exacting than others, with meals provided by willing helpers wherever they stopped, together with endless cups of tea and 'polite conversation', they have about them a touch of Anglican church outings.

'A party of seven of us including lay supporters set out in a converted army truck. We first called at a monastery between Gallo and Metara where we were given tea, and polite conversation was indulged in . . . It had a most attractive atmosphere . . . rather like a spacious eighteenth century farmhouse with its yard and wide verandas . . . and prints here and there on the walls . . . All wore an air of dignified and simple seclusion.'

They travel on to another monastery, Sinimadera, which proves a disappointment.

'New dwellings, new shrines, new (and gracious, how awful!) sculpture and all or most of it in cement. The principal (most hospitable, cheerful and an indefatigable talker) has a passion for having an example of everything mentioned in the Texts in the way of monastic equipment . . . The whole thing was in the style of a child's painted, plaster Noah's ark, and its ugliness was only equalled by the charm and amiability of the people there. More tea . . .'

It was dark when they reached Tissamaharama, an early centre of learning and pilgrimage abandoned about 1500 but now restored. Here there was more tea. As the area was malarial they slept under mosquito nets. Ten miles on through a jungle heavily scented with jasmine bushes, they reach their first objective, a ruined monastery called Magulinahaavihara. Here there are rocks three hundred feet high 'fitted out as cave dwellings, temples and so on. The view from the top was really an Italian primitive come to life – the flat green jungle like a sea all round out of which rose huge, fantastic granite rocks like the bodies of elephants, rounded, grey, enormous and very old. Scattered about almost as if taken out of a box and set there for ornament were isolated hills and mountains, jagged single, twin and triple cones and hogs' backs – to the south the sea and to the north the central massif.'

Yet another ten miles and they reach Cittalapabbata the abandoned settlement for which they had set out. 'The area covering the hills was bigger and more impressive, but the outstanding feature was the tremendous atmosphere surrounding it. . . . It is said to have contained so many saints at one time living there that it became unsuitable for meditation and retreat owing to the crowds which came constantly to see them . . . We spent the night there with a fire to keep off bears. . . At dawn the singing of the birds was like the tuning up of a big orchestra.'

On the return journey they visit a forest hermitage where there are crowds of people and pious slogans attached to the trees. 'As we wandered round looking at the rather Grimm's Fairy Tales cave dwellings we were followed by a party of the public. Eventually we came to the reception room, a deeper, larger cave elegantly white washed and well furnished. Here we had tea amid much bowing down and exchange of politeness . . . Supporters came from all over the place and from Colombo nearly one hundred and seventy miles away to prepare dama (that is, food for the monks). Opportunities to be able to do this are booked up for years ahead. The whole thing – especially such things as appointing a relay of people to fan a statue of the Buddha on hot days – much amused our party and, personally, I found it quaint to say the least.'

They stopped again at Sinimodera for their midday meal. 'Our host was in greater spirits than ever. During ablutions at the well he seized a German hermit of some sixty-odd years and scrubbed his face heartily with soap while he bleated in protest.' They leave with their host 'talking and beaming to the last' as he waves goodbye from the veranda steps.

The rest of the journey was uneventful. A visit to only one other monastery is recorded: '. . . very neat, new and tidy with a very smart new library – more tea and polite conversation. Since then I have not been off the island and have not wanted to go anywhere, unless, perhaps, to retire to Cittalapabbata – but the food problem there is difficult.'

But the calm of the hermitage was disturbed some months later by what must have been a most distressing event: the arrival of Harold Musson's mother, whether in an attempt to persuade her son to leave the monastery or with the notion of embracing Buddhism herself, is not clear. It seems that Musson must have left London, possibly without telling her of his intentions and certainly without giving her his address. Distracted, she wrote to Susan to ask her to send a message to her son through Bertie. Susan included the message in her first letter. He replies that he has delivered the message but it was unnecessary as mother and son were already in touch.

Mrs Musson's visit occurs a year later, probably in December 1949. It seems she may have confided in Susan who may have written to Bertie to warn him of her intentions. In an undated letter, probably written in January 1950, after a long description of the behaviour of the island cats he comments on her visit.

'Mrs Musson has been and returned. I cannot help feeling that all would have been happier if the visit had not taken place. Still, it is difficult to know the workings of one's own mind, let alone that of another. Certain water creatures delight in adorning their shells with other shells, pebbles, and leaves. Sometime they stick on another living creature without regard to its likes or dislikes. In the building up of systems of relationships between people one sometimes observes one building into his or her scheme of things – his or her psychological house or shelter, as it were – the personality of another . . . Anyway I cannot help feeling that while Mrs Musson is very unhappy, she has made herself much more so by insisting (which appears to be the case, only don't say I said so should the question arise) on coming out here, otherwise she would probably not have had the seizure which was at first thought to be a stroke and later diagnosed as "conversion hysteria", I am told. (All this again for your ears alone.) The mind is a very strange thing indeed. No wonder the whole world rushes madly round seeking distraction from the terrors of its own mind (that is the real escapism) and doesn't look inside!'

Even Susan, worldly and far from soft-hearted herself, must have found this view of the affair rather callous, for in his next letter he writes: 'I, too, am sorry for poor Mrs Musson. It seems that a further diagnosis discovered a stroke which has affected the speech centre. Even now she has not fully recovered. "Be an island unto yourself for there is no other refuge." There seems to be an impasse here out of which there is no getting.'

This is the last we hear of Mrs Musson. More strangely, Harold Musson himself is only mentioned again twice in the whole correspondence. Eighteen months later, in answer to an enquiry from Susan, he adds as a postscript to a long letter: 'You asked, by the way, if Harold Musson is still here. Yes, still here.' In a later letter, prompted, perhaps, by a further enquiry, he writes that when he had stated that he was still here, he had meant in Ceylon. 'He has, in fact, moved a hundred and fifty miles away north of Colombo.' That is all.

There are few descriptions of Buddhist ceremonies in the letters. The fullest and most interesting is his account of the funeral of his much revered Sinhalese preceptor in Colombo.

'He was seventy-eight, had a fall last month, broke his hip and died of pneumonia. I went to Colombo when I heard it and he was still conscious when I saw him in one of Colombo's big nursing homes. It was a death in the grand scale of, it appears, a national figure, and it took place in full public. A death of the sort that seems to have been lost in Europe since the eighteenth century. His pupils took turns at recitations round his bed and increasing crowds of people kept coming day and night, some serving soft drinks from time to time and sitting on the floor. As the days went by the visitors grew more important. The ex-prime minister and the Governor General came and the newspapers were full of it. It was a most strange experience to watch someone one has known personally and greatly liked and looked up to, slowly die in the full glare of the public eye.

'After his death he lay in state in the monastery library for four days. Then the body was taken in procession to the burning ground in the afternoon. It was preceded by a single drum that beat a slow, syncopated tapping, like water dripping on to fallen bread fruit leaves, and a single shawm that went on repeating the same three note phrase. The effect was most moving and extraordinarily right. The procession was two miles long with five hundred bhikkhus [monks] and flocks of people carrying banners and flags. The whole length of the streets being lined with split palm shoots and hung with white cotton drapery.

174

'The scene at the burning ground was a Byzantine painting or, perhaps, a Siennese primitive. In the immediate foreground, from where I was, a belt of human figures, blocked in only two colours: yellow-brown bhikkhus and white laity gave the setting a vigorous classical simplicity. Behind them in the middle distance rose two edifices: on the left the hearse in the form of a pavilion or pagoda made of looking-glass columns and gold and white paper: on the right the pyre which was a higher pavilion, a castle with turrets and domes made entirely of white cotton stretched over a frame. The hearse stood out bright and hard against a single big blackish-green tree, but the soft white pyre seemed to fade half into the sky which was a vague pigeon-grey with huge dim cloud-castles half hidden in it. At sunset the pyre was lighted. The upper part went up in flames while people round about flung firewood and oil on to it. Next morning I went with a small party to collect the ashes.'

Another ceremony he attended he found tawdry and the atmosphere, with large crowds, disagreeable. He had set out on an excursion with a Singhalese monk which took them first to Anuradhapura for the anniversary of the arrival of the son of the Emperor Asoka when he came from India to convert the people of Ceylon. 'The great stretches of shady, grassy parks full of majestic ruins were swarming with hundreds of thousands of people. The great shrine, now restored and looking like the dome of St Paul's placed on the ground, smooth and whitewashed and surmounted with a gilt pinnacle, was floodlit. From the terrace on which it stands (crammed with people in every attitude of worship and refreshment-eating, and literally piled with lotus flowers) the great swell of the dome, which hides all but the top of the spire, seemed to hang suspended with the full moon behind it. Impressive.

'From there it is about a quarter of a mile to the sacred Bodhi tree . . . half-way between was a huge temporary open pavilion in the centre of which a kind of roofed ornamental rotunda filled with monks taking part in a non-stop recitation of scriptures which had lasted for a month all day and all night. As they recited amid a blaze of coloured electric fairy lamps, the rotunda rotated slowly and the recitations were laid on through loudspeakers. The effect was peculiar and indigestible . . . I was not sorry to leave Anuradhapura, impressive as the miles of ruins are and the parks and the great lakes and the three enormous stupa domes.' They went on to Mihimtale nine miles away where, according to legend the Emperor's son alighted after his miraculous flight through the air from India. He finds the monastery, seven hundred steps up a granite staircase, 'a rather wretched recent building bordering on hovel architecture – rich and mean, important, hearty and busy, hospitable and worldly.' They spend the next day exploring the ruins.

They set out to walk back to Anuradhapura towards evening by a little frequented jungle track. 'The road for some miles is quite deserted and shut in on both sides by the monotonous jungle – the jungle which is so easy to get into and so hard to get out of. Where visibility is reduced to about ten yards. By day it is hot, airless and dry. There is an uneasy sense of being watched or just observed with indifference or verging, perhaps, on dislike. No Sinhalese will go into it without first breaking off a green branch and hanging it on a tree as a placative measure and there are tree shrines and ant-hill shrines near jungle villages or on lonely roads which no particular religion will own. It is quite quiet except for some occasional hidden bird that warbles off and on with the sweet voice of a concert flute blown by an idiot child, or, rarely, a slight rustle is caused by something always out of sight . . . Sometimes there is a tree with a greasy patch high up on its trunk where elephants rub themselves. Or one comes across an isolated tall tree full of cicadas scraping out loud rhythmic music, as dry and tuneless as a Bartok quartet, to an audience which isn't there. Rarely a troop of monkeys crashes through the branches and fling sticks and abuse at one as they pass, but this only underlines the normal tone of closeness, suspense and commonplaceness.

'Besides ourselves on the road there was only a man and boy and the man's wife in sight. She had quarrelled with him and was walking on far ahead sulking, carrying a child and not looking back while he kept shouting at her to stop, but she only walked faster and said nothing. He was carrying a small, battle-axe-shaped hatchet of the kind used for fighting off attacks by bears.

'The jungle is full of bears. They live on termites mostly which they suck out of termite hills, and honey; but they loathe the sight of man. If a bear sees one, it rushes upon him, screaming horribly, I'm told, and claws out his eyes. They wake up about sunset.

'The sun was, in fact, just going out of sight, and it was very quiet . . . The darkness comes on very quickly. The jungle which mostly dozes by day, under the stupefying sun, wakes up then. Slack strings are tensed and vibrate. Whole orchestras of crickets strike up; things prowl and owls hiccup and cough and fireflies drift up and down. The sense of being observed gets worse. As the sun went down the woman's fear suddenly overcame her anger. She stopped and waited for the man and boy with their axe to catch her up. We left them behind in the darkness. It was some time before we came to the first houses.'

The excursion turned out to be one of the longest he undertook, or, at least, described. Joining up with some other monks in a bus they went down the east coast as far as the centre of the island where they turned inland to visit temples in the neighbourhood of Kandy. 'We spent every night', he concludes, 'in a different monastery and saw many others. I was surprised by the number of monks who live isolated in remote caves in the forest.'

Two years later he tries out cave dwelling for himself, but only for ten days. He does not mention having any companions with him neither does he make a point of being alone which he surely would have done had his stay been quite solitary, nor does it seem likely that the happening he describes at the end of the ten days would have taken place unless other monks had been with him.

'To get to the place I had to go by bus eight miles beyond Hambantola and then walk two miles in the uninhabited jungle to a high rock which stands above the tree tops about one hundred feet. There are three ruined brick shrines on top and a lot of ruined stone buildings on the sides where there are also deep pools of water. At the bottom on one side there are two caves in one of which I stayed. The nearest houses were two miles away along the road. Each night elephants and tortoises and other things left their footprints in the jungle track. I saw a wild deer and some jackals and a very big gorged python under a tree (incredible sight!) and a peacock in flight (there were lots of them screaming rather royally, musically and triumphantly in the jungle). Also I caught a glimpse of a tusker elephant one evening in the dusk. Hornbills in the trees, too, as big as geese (their heads are too big for their bodies and their bodies for their tails so that when they perch on a branch they first topple forward and only right themselves with unseemly antics) and lots of monkeys. At night huge black scorpions would creep out of their houses (holes in the ground) and sit outside their doorsteps waiting for something to happen. In the morning lovely pink-plush mites walked about looking for guidance, alone or one following another or in little files of three or four like large animated wild strawberries . . . There was a most improbable view from the top of the rock, just the view, exactly, that a fly must get when it sits on one of the things in a Palissy-ware plate* – all mossy looking jungle with a complete six or seven mile distant rim just like a plate. Beyond the rim (in an altogether other world, nothing to do with me at all) was the whole range of the Ceylon mountains to the north and east . . . and to the south, over the rim, a small strip of salt-pan and then the ocean . . . My plate, which hypnotized me, was nothing but a mossy mass of jungle crawling with living things (some enormous), ringing with birds, heavily scented with several sorts of jasmine and jungle flowers . . . all the plants blooming away after the rain and trying their best to strangle each other, animals whooping like demons and tearing each other to bits and millions of birds singing away like lunatic angels. Nature seems to me on such occasions like a mad ogress in a flowery cotton-print crinoline frock and spring hat. She is quite horrible, isn't she? and as fascinating as one of her painted vipers is to a painted bird.

'At the end of the ten days about one hundred and fifty people from different places, came flocking together by cars, bullock carts and on foot, and produced a ceremonial meal. Very senior monks came and gave sermons under the neighbouring banyan tree which was the monkey's bedroom at night. After which everyone played at Johnny Crowe's garden for a bit and then went their various ways abandoning the place to the animals.'

Delightful and sometimes alarming descriptions of animals, birds, reptiles and insects occur throughout the letters. The earliest have pages on the behaviour of the cats on the hermitage island. They produce a comment from Susan to which he responds: 'You are right about animal and human behaviour – the parallelism

---

* Shades of the antique shop in the Broad. The ware was made by Palissy in the sixteenth century: plates and dishes and vases, mostly green, and remarkable for being covered with all sorts of objects and creatures, lizards, toads, snakes and foliage in high relief.

works both ways and argues, one would think sometimes, in favour of the notion of rebirth – I don't mean metempsychosis* or anything so concrete or tiresomely immortalistarian [sic] as that, but more in the sense of strains of consciousness that might reproduce themselves in different levels of existence. I don't see why, for instance, some of the people one has met should not be reborn as an ant-hill or did not exist say as a hornet's nest before they became human. Who knows, too, whether the present state of the world is not mostly due to the contents of some termite-hill having contrived to get born into it? And nowadays, too, it is becoming fashionable to talk about the "collective unconscious".'

He claims to have become fairly practised at bottling snakes, including a two-and-a-half foot cobra, in old Horlicks containers, for transportation to a neighbouring uninhabited island.

'We catch on an average two a month, mostly varieties of Kraits, I believe . . . I must confess I personally like snakes and were I alone I would let them be and feed the cobras. There is a very nice and harmless whip snake speckled green and brown who rears up when one meets him and wriggles his neck in an extraordinary way like a Turkish stomach dancer. Rat snakes, six to eight feet long, go about with complete unconcern for one's presence. The other day one climbed a mangrove tree and seized a dozing crane by the foot. There was a fearful uproar among the cranes and the victim escaped. Two days ago, in washing a handkerchief, I found myself washing a two inch grey scorpion mixed up with it. It gave me a lot of trouble getting the soap off it after which I put it in the cinnamon bushes hoping it was none the worse. Kindness to twelve inch centipedes which leap at you and make a rattling noise and remind one of miniature models of the long chains of iron luggage trolleys on the platform of the Gare de Lyon, is admittedly difficult. I bottle them and release them at the far end of the island. The suspected presence of a centipede is, one notes, very inimicable to the preservation of dignity.'

In hot weather he observes that the birds 'sit about with open beaks, look wild . . . with a tendency to shriek madly. One bottle-

---

* Basic to Buddhist doctrine, but not now much believed in by sophisticated Buddhists. A Tibetan lama, of the long established Tibetan colony at Darjeeling, to whom I gave some account of Nānamoli's life had no doubt that he had been born to become a monk as a result of the high spiritual level he had attained to in his previous existence.

green bird with white patches round its eyes and front which makes it look as if it had stuffed its face into a bowl of porridge and let it all run down its shirt, shrieks "Kotoruwa" (coconuts) alternatively from left to right, its whole body vibrating with passion and will go on doing it for hours.'

After climbing Adam's Peak (the highest mountain in Sri Lanka) on the way down he encounters a millipede 'the amiable kind, you know, which rolls itself in a spiral. It was climbing up a tree and was all made of shiny black lacquer rings. Its lemon-yellow legs flowed by in waves. It was quite a foot long and proportionately thick. Also there was a dragon lizard marbled mossy green and brown with a jagged mane and an ivory white rhinoceros horn on the tip of its nose. I met a daddylonglegs today, but not quite the kind one is used to. Though its body and wings were the ordinary size and shape, its legs were a full three inches long, thin as one hundred cotton, gracefully curved and clothed in yellow and white banded football stockings. It was like one of those creatures in Dali's *Temptation of St Anthony*. A product of natural selection? Nonsense! Made by a creator, then? But why not the third possibility, that its family had always been interested in being different and had worked it out long ago for themselves?'

It is not until August 1952 that he first writes of his intention to translate into English some of the texts from the Pali canon. By 1955 he has become so absorbed in the work that he lets almost a whole year pass without writing to Susan. He tells her that somebody wants to publish one book he has translated, originally for his own edification. 'It is the principal commentary on the Tipitala and was written in Ceylon at the time of St Augustine. After a wave of conflicting feelings, I eventually agreed, but that meant typing it, about one thousand pages, and then, of course, in the process altered my style, changed my mind and generally had a distracting time of it. This took from April to October spending all daylight hours every day, typing about five pages a day and revising it. Now someone is reading through it and I have got to compose an introduction . . . I can no longer hide behind the author translated but have to come, as it were, off my fence and actually say something, myself.'

Later he writes that he has put his name in the first letters of each sentence in the preface. It amuses him to see if anyone will notice. 'It represents partly the getting past an obstacle and partly some rather abstruse literary amusement for myself.' Two years later when translating various texts has become his primary undertaking, he describes it as 'a particular kind of soothing occupation like playing a musical instrument and solving mathematical problems'.

Despite his declared ambition to 'obtain to obscurity' he is clearly not too put out when someone writes to tell him that 'my remaining here, coupled with translating Pali, is creating a sort of legendary reputation in Colombo. Now if that were so, I think it would be fine; for then I might travel even further by letting my legendary, or otherwise, self go and live in, say, Colombo while I stay here without it. I think we could get on very well at a distance; we could write to each other, of course, occasionally, but not depend on each other in the rather futile way we do.'

Although from 1952 onwards his translation work so absorbed him (one rather wonders how much time was left for the meditation which took up most of his early days at the hermitage and which he had declared, along with the practice of renunciation, to be the main object of living a monk's life), he still went on occasional outings or pilgrimages. It was on one such in March 1960 that, at the age of fifty-five and apparently in sound health, he was struck down by a fatal heart attack.

Here would seem a fitting point in this sketch of his life to quote from the tribute paid to him by the Venerable Nanyaponika in his introduction to the posthumously published *A Thinker's Notebook*.

'What was known of the monk life of the Venerable Nanãmoli to a wider public in Ceylon and abroad, was his outstanding scholarly work in translating from the original Pali into lucid English . . . His translations showed the highest standard of careful and critical scholarship and a keen and subtle mind, philosophically trained. His work in this field is a lasting contribution to Buddhist studies.

'It was characteristic of him that he had limited his publication to that scholarly field, so that his "public image" was that of an able scholar and exemplary monk, which left him enough of his cherished "obscurity".

'Very few knew, or even suspected, those other facets of his rich and profound mind, which in the present volume appear in such an astonishing variety . . . Yet there were still other layers of his mind (and still not the deepest) without which the personality presented by this book and in his scholarly work would be incomplete and misleading. These other features of his character, however, manifested themselves only in his way of life and in his human relationships. From his unrelenting realistic world-view, as appearing in his note books undeceived by the deceptions and self-deceptions of life and our own minds – a reader could possibly gain the impression of a harsh if not cynical character with a rather contemptuous view of mankind. But this would be very far from the deep humanity and friendly composure of his nature which made his self-effacing reticence still more unobtrusive. He had a natural affinity with the Buddha's detachment as well as his compassionate outlook . . . His friendliness and compassion were unsentimental and undemonstrative, but of a simple human warmth. His quiet and friendly smile will be unforgettable to his companions . . . The simplicity and frugality of a Buddhist monk came quite natural to him . . . In the Buddha's teaching on reality and man's situation in it, he found fresh inspiration for his own thought, and the Buddha's practical path to deliverance being the solution to the human predicament, was the guiding and directing force of his inner life.'

I do not think there is anything in the preceding extracts taken from his letters from Ceylon, with the possible exception of his rather heartless attitude to Mrs Musson's visit and his strange reticence about what had become of Harold Musson, which detract from Nanyaponika's tribute. Indeed, there is a most sympathetic aspect of his character, untouched on in the introduction, as revealed in his keen observation and aesthetic appreciation of the natural world around him and his readiness to preserve the lives of creatures not merely repellant to most people, but lethally dangerous to handle, as in the care with which (here, surely, a hint of St Francis!) he cleaned the soap off the scorpion inadvertently caught up in his laundry.

Sadly, however, there proved to be much in the letters, whole pages, indeed, which not only tend to reproduce and reinforce the unfavourable impression which Nanyaponika admitted might be drawn from a reading of the *Notebooks*, but are at odds with those qualities the tribute so warmly extols: his detachment, compassion, self-effacement and dedication to obscurity.

After the first three letters, short and hastily written, the contents of which have already been touched upon, the correspondence takes off into those densely-written, many paged missives which were to be dispatched, with only rare lapses of more than a few months, until shortly before his death. What is striking about them is how different they are in tone and content from those written from the Isle of Man and Italy, and how changed the personality of their author appears to have been by the two years he spent in England.

There are several possible influences which may have helped to bring about this change. One was the effect of working at the BBC where, probably with justification, he felt himself to be intellectually superior to his colleagues, and was contemptuous of the prevailing atmosphere of petty intrigue: another was his close friendship with Musson, although, apart from their addiction to abstruse metaphysical discussion and their mutual attraction to Buddhism, there is nothing in the letters to indicate how their intimacy in London may have affected him, or why it should have depreciated after their arrival in Ceylon. More important, perhaps was the influence of Susan herself and the weekends at Stanton. When he admits to the strength of his regrets at separation from his friends, he declares his ties to be centred on Stanton and Beckley, but it is always to Susan that he writes. When she asks him if she can give his address to the Feildings, he replies: 'Of course I have no objection to Basil and Peggy having my address. I have not written to them (for selfish reasons, if you like) because I want to write as few letters as possible and because I might find it difficult at times to know what to write about. It is better not to go to a party if one has not suitable clothes to go in, though this has nothing to do with one's regard for those whose party it is.'

In his early letters from the Isle of Man he had been desperately eager for news of the Beckley circle, whereas now it is for news of friends to whom Susan has introduced him while he was in England, some scarcely more than acquaintances, that he has an insatiable appetite, protesting when she hints of some new twist in relationships that she has not told him enough. He takes a keen interest in Susan's relations with her daughter, Valerie. Responding to Susan's complaint that she has learnt through a friend that Valerie has been deceiving her about her sentiments towards her young man, he comments: 'If she is putting it on, it shows considerable ability on which she should really be complimented, although it is scandalous that it should be at your expense.'

However impressive his detachment may have appeared to his fellow monks, the correspondence shows, in respect to the past, that it was flawed; for whatever else he may have succeeded in renouncing, his yearning for gossip from England is so strong that he can write: 'I am tantalized by your saying that you have a lot more to tell me and I am full of curiosity about S—, etc; write and tell me everything about everybody.'

As to compassion, he showed little towards Mrs Musson, nor does it surface often elsewhere in the letters other than in cool expressions of sympathy or regret. The attempted suicide of a former colleague in London he finds 'interesting because there is something poignantly modern in the strident incongruity of the mixture of champagne and coal gas, and something so personally right that even that should fail.' Of the death of a Dutch friend with whom he went on a holiday in the Netherlands shortly before leaving for Ceylon, he has nothing to say except that his attitude to art was encyclopaedic and he had no genuine appreciation of painting. When he hears that of a cousin of Susan's has been left by his wife, his comment is vicious. 'The story sounds too true to be good. You should keep in touch with her because it will be most interesting to hear a first hand account of hell, for she will certainly go there.' As it turned out, she outlived Susan, who ended her life suffering from the hell of a mind-incapacitating stroke, to become a distinguished art historian, remaining on the friendliest terms with her former husband.

When Susan writes that Geoffrey Dennis, who so befriended him in the Isle of Man and who was responsible for requesting his release from the army to join the BBC, has asked for news of him, he feels it necessary to explain why he never introduced him to her. Gratuitously and without a hint of gratitude for what he owed him, he gives an unrelentingly disparaging account of his character, listing among his defects, 'his bad taste and vulgarity of

manner, aggressive humility, restless hunting after spiritual satisfaction and venomous wrangling with his wife over their divorce'.
He ends by telling Susan he has no objection to her letting him
know that he is in Ceylon.

That harsh and contemptuous view of mankind of which
Nanyaponika warned, is expressed in the letters more strongly
and frequently than in the *Notebook*. It was, perhaps, reinforced
by his study of existentialism which, itself, may have been encouraged (as seems likely from what we were to learn later) by tea-time
table-talk with the German monks at Doanduwa. After describing
it as a dismal, though rather convincing, philosophy of pessimism
('we are in hell and at cross purposes and there is no way out'), he
asks Susan to send him two works by Sartre, which were left in his
flat, and for any others more recently published. A reading of
L'Etre et le néant he admits to leaving him somewhat shattered.
'While it is a difficult and forbidding book, it is the most
convincing philosophical treatise I have ever read. Still, I would
not recommended anyone to read it.'

Along with his existentialist studies his interest in the state of
the world revives and his early resolution to stop reading newspapers is abandoned. His reaction to events is predictably, and
often with good reason, pessimistic, but while he deplores them he
does not conceal that they reassure him of the rightness of his
decision to withdraw into the monastic life. He sees himself as
'sitting on the fence, but such a small and obscure one that it is
unlikely that anyone will bother to uproot it'.

The news that Susan's son, Robert, has become a convert to
Catholicism and, later, that he is to enter the Dominican order
revives his old prejudice against the Catholic Church. The only
attraction it has ever had for him is in 'its decorative grandeur,
emotional glamour and thrill of mystery'. But he has 'always been
unable to perform the sacrifice of reason on the altar of emotion
which the Church demands, mainly because it disgusts me'. He
cannot stomach St Thomas Aquinas' philosophy which 'seems to
me to have an alien, oppressive and unsatisfactory, smartish taste'.
While he finds papal infallibility and the bodily assumption 'not
only absurd but in bad style', he is strongly against the taking of
irrevocable vows as imposed by the Church. In Buddhism no such
vows are demanded. After reading the Ceylon letters and with

Nanyaponika's eulogy still in mind, I felt that the subject of whom I had set out to write this account had developed two quite different personalities: the one, hard-hearted, cynical, astringent, gossipy and not without malice (so very different from the character we had known or thought we had known in the past – withdrawn in his shy friendliness and retiringly modest though so erudite and many-gifted); the other (not at all at odds with what we might have then conceived – for there was always a touch of the monastic about him – as his eventual destiny), the exemplary monk and dedicated scholar only breaking off from his elucidation of obscure texts to make pilgrimages to remote jungle sanctuaries, impressing those he travelled or met with, by his piety and equable temperament, and always observant of the nature around him while equally sympathetic to whatever creatures, commonplace, exotic or even venomous, he encountered.

When we visited Sri Lanka in 1982 we had already learnt in Bangkok of Nanãmoli's renown as a Pali scholar and translator, but it was not until some years later, after Susan's death, that Basil lent me the letters he had written to her during the war and from Doanduwa. Certainly our visit to the Venerable Nanyaponika in his forest hermitage was the most rewarding event of our stay.

A few days after our meeting with him, armed with the letter of introduction he had given, we set out from Colombo to visit the island hermitage at Doanduwa. The sixty-mile ribbon of pot-holed and dangerously-cambered tarmac running along the west coast between Colombo and Galle was jammed with traffic of all kinds from vast lorries to ox carts and bicycles, through which the driver of the taxi we had hired, drove with alarming aggressiveness.

The lake at Doanduwa reaches at its western extremity to within a few yards of the road. There were several fishing boats pulled up on the shore, but when we asked one of the fishermen to take us out to the island, he refused, explaining that tourists were forbidden to visit the hermitage and that he would get into serious trouble with the monks. It was only when we showed him our letter from Nanyaponika, addressed to the abbot, that he reluctantly agreed.

The lake is about two miles long with the island in the middle. Starting out towards it, had we already read Nanãmoli's letters, we would have seen that its setting had changed little since his description of it written some thirty years before. Despite the proximity of the tourist-infested fringe along the coast, no new buildings had sprung up along its shores and no speed-boats disturbed its glassy surface. The low hills rising steeply out of the unbroken jungle were still elegantly tufted with coconut palms. All that was missing was the sense of remoteness remarked on by Nanãmoli, for if there were still the thumping of coconuts being pounded for their fibre or the constant beating of drums 'in complicated rhythms', they would have been drowned by the noise of the traffic on the Colombo road.

Nearing the island we saw on the shore to one side, within easy rowing distance of it, a temple with numerous outbuildings, the settlement, no doubt, to which our hermit had, as we were to read later in the letters, made occasional trips as breaks from meditation or translating from the Pali. Our boatman headed for a gap in the ring of mangrove trees which hedged in the island. Steering through it under arched branches he sidled the boat against a wooden landing stage. As we got out he kept looking round so nervously that we feared he would not obey our instructions to wait for us. A path tunnelled through the trees, wound up from the shore. We had just started along it when a Sinhalese, evidently a lay brother, came hurrying to meet us. We held out our letter defensively, but he did not bother to look at it, explaining that a message had already been received from Nanyaponika and the monks were expecting us. Pointing to the boatman he asked if we had paid him for bringing us over. When we replied that we had agreed on a modest sum, he turned on the man with a spate of abuse in Sinhalese which left him cowering at the bottom of his boat. He had no right to ask for anything, we were told. On no account should we think of paying him.

The tunnelled path opened on to an area of level ground on which a wooden hut with a corrugated iron roof stood out from the partially cleared jungle. This, our guide told us, was the refectory where the monks would be waiting to receive us.

The hut was rather dark inside and austerely furnished with a table and chairs at its centre from which four youngish looking monks (shaved heads make age difficult to determine) rose to give us a friendly welcome. They spoke fluent English with a German accent. We were presented to the abbot who was sitting by himself in an armchair in one corner. As he was Sinhalese and spoke no English we were only able to exchange polite bows and smiles. We explained to the others that we had known Nanāmoli well many years before when he had been living near Oxford, that we had corresponded with Nanyaponika about him and were naturally interested in seeing the place in which he had spent the remaining years of his life after leaving England.

One of the monks offered to show us his 'cell'. It was only a short distance away along a path which zigzagged through the semi-jungle. Though quite small and sparsely furnished the hut offered an agreeable enough retreat for anyone of a solitary disposition. Next we were shown where he was buried, an unmarked patch of cleared ground under a tangle of tropical greenery.

On our return to the refectory we found tea with lemon awaiting us. We sat down at the table with the monks, two of whom had been long enough at the hermitage to have known Nanāmoli. From all that Nanyaponika had told us of his dedication to the monastic life and his international renown as a Pali scholar, we assumed that his memory would be sufficiently revered by his brother monks for those who had known him personally or even only by repute to be interested in hearing something of his English background and early life. Accordingly I told them all that I knew of his upbringing on Tresco and of how, despite having received little formal eduaction, he had been accepted as a student at Oxford. I went on to describe how, when living at Beckley (what another world it seemed with its fine furniture and topiary garden from this tin-roofed shed in its jungle setting!), he had astounded all who met him by his erudition, gift for languages and the varied skills in which, though self-taught, he had excelled. They listened politely, but I sensed that they were not much interested in what I was telling them, so I let my account of Bertie, as we had known him, trail lamely off. They smiled but asked no questions and made no comments until one of them conceded, though rather dismissively, that he had been an able and dedicated scholar.

In the silence which followed we drank our tea and were encouraged to refill our cups. As there appeared nothing more to be said, I was about to suggest that it was time for us to leave when I was asked by one of the monks, and the others perked up as they waited for my answer, if I had known the friend he had come out with. They were clearly disappointed when I admitted that I had never met Musson and knew nothing about him. But now my own curiosity was aroused and, once reminded of him, I was prompted to enquire why, if he was still in the community, he was not present at the tea-table.

If a little dismayed by their cool attitude to the memory of poor Bertie, had I been a friend of Harold Musson I would have been heartened by their reply, for they spoke of him with the mixture of enthusiasm and reverence usually reserved by the faithful for a guru or near-saint. Revealing that they were existentialists, they told us how much they owed to him for his interpretation of that philosophy in Buddhist terms, and how they acknowledged him as their continuing inspiration. Some years before, committed to the exacting demands of his faith, he had withdrawn to a remote part of the island where he had built himself a hut beside a jungle track a mile from the nearest village. There with great courage and endurance, a true anchorite, he had dedicated himself to a life of solitude and meditation, relying on the village people to fill his begging bowl with sufficient food to sustain him. After some years, he had developed cancer. Declining any form of medication he had set himself by the practice of meditation alone to arrest the progress of the disease and overcome the pain it inflicted on him. He had had friends in Colombo who visited him from time to time, but he refused the medicines they brought until one such visitor managed to persuade him to accept a bottle of pain-killers. For a time he put them aside and did not use them until, finally, when the pain became insupportable and he found it impossible to continue meditating, he took all the pills at one go and killed himself.

A good death, calm and resigned whatever the suffering, is considered by Buddhists to be of the greatest importance, especially for a monk, to ensure the spirit a propitious onward passage. Of all ways of dying suicide is considered the worst.

Horrified by the manner of Musson's death, the hierarchy in Colombo had reacted with inordinate asperity. We were not told what form this took, but it seemed likely that he had been refused the full burial rights customarily accorded to a monk.

His existentialist followers had been so disillusioned by their behaviour that they were considering leaving the island. They had heard that there was a growing interest in Buddhism in Europe and wanted to know if this was true of England. We were able to tell them that there was a Theravada temple in London and that we knew of a flourishing monastery in the country. They appeared encouraged by this and we parted from them with a friendly exchange of the ritual smiles and bows.

We found our boatman still waiting for us. As we recrossed the lake, the noise of the traffic growing steadily louder, we pondered the contrast between Nanyaponika's heartfelt tribute to Nanāmoli and the casual regard in which his memory was held by his brother monks at the Hermitage. With our own recollections of him in mind and the admiration and affection we had felt for him, Nanyaponika's adulation had not come as a surprise. That the monks, younger and with their existentialist leanings, should have lacked the perception to see in him more than a dry scholar, was understandable. What had really astonished us was what they had told us about Harold Musson. Known only through the Feildings' disparaging description of him, had we learned before our visit of his decision to become a lone hermit in the jungle, we might have taken it as a theatrical gesture; but from the account we had just been given, especially of his death, there could be no doubt of the sincerity of his resolve and the endurance he had shown in carrying it out.

When preparing this sketch of Osbert Moore's life, I read the letters he had written from Doanduwa. I found it difficult to explain his failure to mention anything of the friend he travelled out with and together with whom he had been initiated into the same monastic order, until in answer to a direct enquiry and then with evident reluctance giving only the minimal information. Even if he may have questioned Musson's motives in choosing to live as an anchorite, why in his reply to Susan did he confine himself to the bare statement that he was living a hundred and fifty miles away? Was it, possibly, because he felt a weakness in his own position, since after all that he had written of his desire for a hermit's life, he had been content to stay on at Doanduwa, appreciative of his growing fame as a Pali scholar while enjoying the frugal but easy going and, when he felt the need of it, companiable atmosphere of the community?

At the time these questions did not trouble us, but even if we had already read the letters which gave rise to them, we would not have been any less moved to have seen the island retreat in its beautiful tropical setting where Bertie, whom we had so much esteemed and so regretfully remembered from Beckley days, had passed in meditation and abstruse Theravada studies the last eleven years of his life.